Conversations
on Purpose
for women

Pathway to Purpose™ Series

Pathway to Purpose™ for Women

Conversations on Purpose for Women

Praying for Purpose for Women

Pathway to Purpose™ for Women Abridged Audio CD

Pathway to Purpose™ for Women Personal Journal

Conversations
on Purpose
for women

10 appointments
that will help you
discover God's plan
for your life

KATIE BRAZELTON

GRAND RAPIDS, MICHIGAN 49530 USA

We want to hear from you. Please send your comments about this
book to us in care of zreview@zondervan.com. Thank you.

ZONDERVAN™

Conversations on Purpose for Women
Copyright © 2005 by Katherine F. Brazelton

Requests for information should be addressed to:
Zondervan, *Grand Rapids, Michigan 49530*

ISBN 0-7394-5336-X

Interior design by Beth Shagene

Printed in the United States of America

To the women leaders, teachers,
and staff of Saddleback Church;
to my mentors, prayer partners,
accountability partners, role models, and best friends;
to my LifePlan clients and protégés;
and to all those women who want God
to use them in a powerful way.

I thank you for what I have learned
from each of you about faith, surrender,
and purpose.

CONTENTS

Part Three
SEEING THE BIGGER PICTURE

Appendixes

HOW TO USE THE PATHWAY TO PURPOSE™ SERIES

All three Pathway to Purpose™ books work together to enhance your journey as you discover your unique God-given calling.

Pathway to Purpose for Women, the main book in the series, shows you how to connect your to-do list, your passions, and God's purposes for your life. How do you live through—see through—the *ordinary* when you yearn for your own *significant* purpose? Discover how God has uniquely designed you and used your life experiences to prepare you for your specific calling. If you can read only one of the three books, this is the one to read. (This book also is available as an Abridged Audio CD.)

- *Personal use*—Each chapter ends with a Bible exploration and personal questions.
- *Small Group and Retreat use*—See the Group Discussion Guide in the back of the book.

Conversations on Purpose for Women is designed for the reader of *Pathway to Purpose for Women* who wants to go deeper. This workbook encourages you to choose a Purpose Partner and make ten appointments with each other. Enjoy conversation starters, Scripture verses, questions, and specific self-assessment exercises that help you unpack God's unique purpose for your life, from an initial sneak preview to the most challenging steps of your journey.

- *Personal use with your Purpose Partner*—Find a partner and enjoy fellowship and growth while exploring God's specific life purposes together.
- *Small Group and Retreat use*—Work through the book as a small group, women's Sunday school class, or in a retreat setting by dividing into groups of three to four maximum and completing and discussing the exercises at paced intervals.

Praying for Purpose for Women is a sixty-day prayer experience that guides you as you ask God to reveal your life's purposes. You will discover insights from modern-day role models and biblical characters, specific questions to ask yourself as you seek God's answers, and an eye-opening analysis of your life patterns and purposes.

- *Personal use*—This book can be used by itself as a daily devotional. However, if you use it as a devotional while reading *Pathway to Purpose for Women*, your whole experience will be deepened and solidified.
- *Retreat use*—Ideal for a solitude retreat. Women can work through the book at their own pace during the weekend. On the last day together, they can pair up to discuss their findings, regardless of how far they got in the book.

Also available:

Pathway to Purpose for Women Personal Journal

As you search for and discover God's unique purpose for your life, it is important to record "what the Lord has done" in your family life, your personal life, and your ministry life. Each page in this companion book to *Pathway to Purpose for Women* will guide your journaling and allow you to reflect on how God is directing you on the pathway of your life.

And I urge you to consider this supplemental material:

The Purpose-Driven® Life

My dear pastor, Rick Warren, wrote this phenomenal bestseller, which sends up a clarion call for people to live out God's five purposes for their lives. If you haven't read his book yet, I highly recommend it. I also recommend that your church go through the powerful 40 Days of Purpose campaign.

Series Foreword

In 1997 Katie facilitated a two-day LifePlan for me and I found the experience highly significant—a turning point!

Up until then, I had been frustrated and confused about my spiritual gifts and goals, and unclear about the contribution my life would make for God's kingdom. Through Katie's firm-yet-gentle guidance, I viewed my life with new eyes and discovered a greater appreciation for God. Using large sheets of butcher paper hanging in her living room, we traced the path I had taken from childhood, and it became crystal-clear that God had been directing me at every point. I was humbled and convinced of his love for me. Things I knew intellectually moved from my head to my heart, and I was able to find joy and meaning in pain I had experienced.

The Holy Spirit used Katie to open my eyes to attitudes, sins, and wrong desires that I had been holding on to, and through a healing prayer time, I was able to release them. After reviewing the past and confirming the present, she drew from me the blue-sky dreams I had for my future . . . dreams I had been afraid to say out loud. In Katie's warm, gracious, encouraging presence, I invited God to use me in ways I never expected, never thought possible, and never even dared to hope. Our tears mingled as she affirmed God's call on my life, her belief that God had allowed the pain for his good purposes, and her faith in my ability to actually fulfill the God-inspired goals and dreams articulated in our time together.

Years later, many of those lessons still affect my daily life. God has taken me up on my offer to be used by him, and though the task often seems more than I can handle, I think back to those hours of breakthrough and am reassured that HE is directing my steps and HE will finish the work.

Katie brings this same warmth, gentle firmness, deep conviction, and passion for God to her books. You may never have the privilege of calling her "friend" as I do, but through her writings, you will find a dear companion for your spiritual journey.

Kay Warren
Saddleback Church
November 2004

Part One

The
Power *of*
Conversations
on Purpose

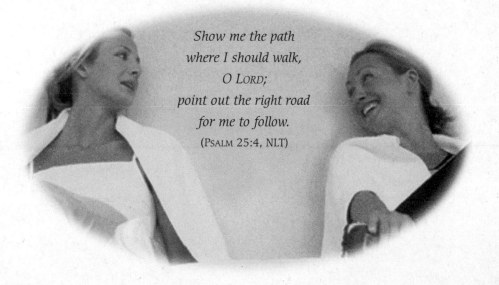

Show me the path
where I should walk,
O LORD;
point out the right road
for me to follow.
(PSALM 25:4, NLT)

Understanding
the Power of the Process

Your eyes saw my unformed body. All the days ordained
for me were written in your book before one of them came to be.
(PSALM 139:16)

All people seek purpose in their lives. Our human nature drives us to search for meaning and significance, to believe that life matters. That's why my pastor, Rick Warren, touched such a deep nerve across the globe in his bestselling books, *The Purpose-Driven Church* and *The Purpose-Driven Life*. In them he explains the five purposes for the church and for our lives, based on the Great Commandment (Matthew 22:37–40) and the Great Commission (Matthew 28:19–20): fellowship, discipleship, ministry, evangelism, and worship.

I have personally experienced the discovery, hope, focus, and freedom of living with purpose, as the Bible describes. And through years of serving and teaching women, I have seen many of them also embrace their life purposes.

But perhaps, like me, you have wondered, "Once I discover my purposes, how will this change me? How does change—progress—happen in my life? How do I move from merely hearing new information to actually thinking, perceiving, and behaving in new ways? How can I apply the principles of God's purposes in my life? How do I connect the dots between *living amidst* the details of my life and *living out* God's purposes for my life?"

This workbook will answer these questions. Filled with conversation starters, Scripture verses, comments from role models, and self-assessment exercises, it's a tool to help you live the life God intends for you to live—asking him to reveal *his* plan, doing it *his* way in *his* timing, because *he* is God of all. If you try to demand or invent answers because you are tired of not having any answers, or if you try to get ahead of God in your planning, you will miss his best for your life. Instead, patiently let his Holy Spirit give you answers through prayer, Scripture, reflection, and conversation with another Christian woman as you progress through this book.

An Overview: Where We're Headed

After I explain some basics in this chapter, the real fun begins. Part 2 will take you through six carefully planned conversations with a Purpose Partner (more on her in a bit). You will be asked to do approximately forty-five minutes of preparation in your workbook prior to each conversation, so that your time with your Purpose Partner is spent discussing your answers, not reading and writing while she watches you deeply ponder your life. The best advice you can live by during the conversations is to have fun, trust the process, and trust the Holy Spirit. The final "conversation" in this section is to take what I call a laughter break: to go somewhere with your Purpose Partner for the distinct purpose of *not* thinking about purpose, but enjoying each other's company. Relaxation, pacing yourself, and friendship are key elements of your journey.

Part 3 will surprise you by revealing logical vision out of what may have seemed random exercises in Part 2. In three additional conversations you will analyze the data bits you have been storing up in your workbook, thus allowing you to draw some conclusions about God's general and distinct purposes for your life.

The most important thing you can do is to pray for your complete surrender to God's will by the end of the book. Other than that, just keep following the book's directions, week by week, without trying to figure out how each step contributes to the whole process as you go along.

Unleashing the Power

I like to call this introductory chapter the *power* chapter for three reasons. First, it explains the power of the pen in moving your ideas onto paper. Second, it discusses the primary power of God who gives perspective about his plan for your life. Third, it talks about the power of two women working together through prayerfully guided conversations!

Power of the Pen

As you jot down your answers to workbook questions during your private preparation time, you will notice a budding clarity over the weeks. Without this process of putting pen to paper, your ideas likely would stay jumbled up inside your head. Expect your written answers to shock you at times and delight you at other times. Write whatever comes to mind first. There are no right or wrong answers, so go with the flow!

Power of a Godly Perspective

You gain new perspective when you climb to the top of a mountain to view landscape impossible to see from ground level. Similarly, God can use this workbook as a vantage point to help you see your life as a whole, allowing you to spot patterns and trends about how you operate. This new primary perspective will encourage you to decide objectively if you are happy with what you see, and if you're not, to ask yourself what you're going to do about it.

An important part of gaining a godly perspective about your life's purpose is to take stock of what you have to work with. That's the step successful organizations take before they make a critical decision, launch a strategy, or invest time, money, energy, and resources on any proposed program.

So in Conversations #1–10 you will take stock of who you are, where you've been, what's important to you, and the resources you have available to complete your part in God's larger story. You may be surprised during different sessions to learn:

- How much hurt you've survived
- How talented you are
- How often you have kept God at a distance

- How fear is blocking you from taking action
- How a taste of significance has made you hunger for more
- How God would like you to dream bigger dreams for his glory

You will begin to notice whether you have slipped into dangerous habits, perhaps procrastination, dishonesty, comparing yourself to others, bragging, or the "impostor syndrome" of being afraid that you will be *found out* in some regard. Such obstacles can prevent you from living out God's best plan for your life. But once you recognize these things as weighty, unnecessary baggage, you can ask God to help you unload them from your life to free you for the rest of your journey.

Power of Conversation

Great power is always unleashed whenever two Christian women sit down to prayerfully focus on one single concept for an uninterrupted hour-and-a-half meeting. Now, multiply that times ten appointments!

In this book, we'll refer to those two Christian women—you and your friend—as Purpose Partners.

What is a Purpose Partner? A Purpose Partner is a Christian woman who is willing to invest in you emotionally and spiritually, because she longs to see you used by God. She will walk alongside you, listen to you, encourage you, and help you listen to God about his purposes for your life.

Why do you need a Purpose Partner? God did not intend for us to be lone rangers. He wants us to lean on him and on one another to grow. In 1 Corinthians 3:6, Paul writes, "I planted the seed, Apollos watered it, but God made it grow." Did you notice something important in that verse? God caused the growth, but he used others in the body of Christ to plant, water, and nurture that growth. His Word also tells us that there is great power in two people working together:

> Two people can accomplish more than twice as much as one;
> they get a better return for their labor. If one person falls,
> the other can reach out and help. But people who are alone
> when they fall are in real trouble.

(ECCLESIASTES 4:9-10, NLT)

What should you look for in a Purpose Partner? The two most important qualifications for a Purpose Partner are personal faith in Jesus Christ and a life of love. As you can imagine, the more spiritually and emotionally mature she is, the better. Ideally, she is a woman of prayer, integrity, confidentiality, and vulnerability.

Your Purpose Partner needs to be healed or healing from any crises she might have had, and she must be seeking peacefulness in her life in order for you to get maximum benefit from your time together. If she is having difficulty healing or if she is not seeking peace, I encourage you to choose a different Purpose Partner or to postpone the exercises.

There are three potential traps to be aware of in your search for a Purpose Partner. First, it may not be wise to choose your best friend, who may be too close to you to have a fresh, broad perspective. You may need a new voice in your life, someone who can be much more objective.

The second trap is to search for the ideal woman who "has arrived." I'll save you some time. That woman doesn't exist; she is a figment of wild imagination! Instead, look for someone who has seen some struggle in her life and knows the depth of God's love through trials. Choose someone who can admit that her spiritual life is not perfect, but who attempts daily to become more Christlike.

The third trap is that a married woman may unwittingly decide to choose a man as her Purpose Partner. Please hear my heart on this: Because of the deep bonding that usually takes place between conversants, I've found it best for a married woman to ask another Christian woman to guide her through the exercises. (And, as I mentioned with the first trap, best friends—that includes husbands—may not offer a fresh perspective.) Of course, a single woman could ask an *unattached* godly man to guide her through the exercises—assuming, of course, that he's willing to listen to that much detail!

A Purpose Partner is not a therapist, a preacher, or a teacher. Purpose Partnering is not a substitute for therapy. It is not about fixing you. It is about someone listening to you and encouraging you.

How do you find a Purpose Partner? Ask God to bring to mind the name of a Christian woman who might be willing to join you on this adventure. Pray specifically, as you look through your list of contacts. And expect

God to answer you. He is eager to give you the good gift of the Holy Spirit, who can share wisdom with you through your godly friends:

> *Ask and it will be given to you; seek and you will find; knock and the*
> *door will be opened to you. For everyone who asks receives; he who*
> *seeks finds; and to him who knocks, the door will be opened. Which*
> *of you, if his son asks for bread, will give him a stone? Or if he asks*
> *for a fish, will give him a snake? If you, then, though you are evil,*
> *know how to give good gifts to your children, how much more will*
> *your Father in heaven give good gifts to those who ask him!*
>
> (MATTHEW 7:7-11)

Once you have found a Purpose Partner, fill in the contact information asked for on page 21 so that you will have it readily available.

How will these conversations work? How you proceed is up to you, because there are two ways that you and your Purpose Partner can operate. You can choose a mentor-protégé model to focus only on your life purpose, or you can both go through the exercises in a mutual coaching relationship. Regardless, you will each need your own workbook to review or complete the exercises in preparation for your time together. Whatever model you select, the "Purpose Partner Tips" appendix on pages 133–135 is a useful resource. You may also download the "Purpose Partner Tips" at www.pathwaytopurpose.com.

Decide where the two of you will meet, how often, and for how long. Because there are ten conversations of approximately an hour and a half each, it may seem logical for you to meet once a week for ten weeks, but that schedule is up to you and your Purpose Partner. You can record the date for each meeting in the space provided on page 21.

What follow-up is expected? None is expected. None is required. All follow-up conversations will be a bonus round!

So enlist a partner, prepare for the first conversation as described in the "Wrapping Up" section on page 22, and enjoy the process together! And may God nudge you gently along his pathway to purpose.

My Purpose Partner's Vital Statistics

Name: Robin Hebbel

Address: 1236 Leeds Avenue

Home phone number: 970-252-1569

Mobile phone number: 970-275-2521

Email address: hebbel01@msn.com

Birthday: Feb 3

Our Conversation Appointments

Conversation #1: April 6

Time: 1:00 Place: Robins House

Conversation #2:

Time: Place:

Conversation #3:

Time: Place:

Conversation #4:

Time: Place:

Conversation #5:

Time: Place:

Conversation #6:

Time: Place:

Conversation #7:

Time: Place:

Conversation #8:

Time: Place:

Conversation #9:

Time: Place:

Conversation #10:

Time: Place:

Wrapping Up

CLOSE YOUR READING TODAY IN CONVERSATION WITH GOD:

Dear God, thank you for guiding me into this method of cooperating with you to learn more about your purposes for my life. I appreciate the power of the conversational process I am about to undertake. I believe that writing my answers, challenging my current perspective, and listening to your Holy Spirit speaking through Scripture and a Purpose Partner will help me immensely. Thank you that I will not have to journey down this path on my own, but that you will hand-pick just the right Purpose Partner for me. Make it clear whom I should invite on this adventure with me. In Jesus' name, I pray. Amen.

BEFORE YOUR FIRST CONVERSATION:

- Your advance preparation each week will allow you to move more quickly through the material and spend your time with your Purpose Partner in actual conversation. Prior to your first meeting, please read the chapter and complete the exercises in Conversation #1.
- Pray diligently that your first conversation with your Purpose Partner will be meaningful. Spend time throughout the week praising God for who he is and for all he has done for you thus far. Thank him in advance for the miracles he is going to perform in your life, as you ask for his daily and long-term purposes to be revealed to you.

Part Two

Purposeful
Appointments

As iron sharpens iron,
a friend sharpens a friend.
(PROVERBS 27:17, NLT)

PURPOSE PARTNER COMMITMENT

We, _____*Jill*_____ and _____*Robin*_____,
(Print your name)   (Print your Purpose Partner's name)

do commit with each other to do the following:

- Base all our decisions made during our time together on Scripture.
- Invite the Holy Spirit to fill us with his truth during this ten-week relationship.
- Pray daily for each other.
- Be prepared for each conversation.
- Treat our Purpose Partner conversations as a priority in our schedules, including being prompt to all sessions.
- Share openly and honestly with each other.
- Treasure confidentiality.
- Love each other unconditionally, as Christ first loved us.
- Be accountable to each other for ten conversations.
- End our sessions on time.

Your Signature _____*KJ Donley*_____ Date *3/29/10*

Purpose Partner's Signature _____ Date _____

ASSESSING YOUR READINESS FOR MORE PURPOSE

Open Your Time Together in Conversation with God: *Dear God, today we ask for your wisdom, leading, and insight in regard to our Purpose Partner Commitment and the Self-Assessment about Purpose, as well as the exercises about our characteristics and relationships. We know that you are the only one who can give us the answers we are seeking, and we trust you to tell us whatever you want us to know at this time. In Jesus' name, we pray. Amen.*

Just for Fun: Share something interesting about your family or a little-known fact about yourself.

TODAY'S FIRST TOPIC: PURPOSE PARTNER COMMITMENT

Review and sign the Purpose Partner Commitment on the facing page.

Today's Second Topic: Self-Assessment about Purpose

As you begin this ten-week journey in earnest, read through the assessment below. These are descriptions of four types of women, each representing a common perception of how many women feel about their life purpose. These categories are not absolutes but, rather, shades of gray. Which woman best describes you at this point? Check that box and briefly describe why. Feel free to list an entirely new category that may better describe how you are feeling!

Self-Assessment about Purpose

☑ **The No-Clue Woman** says, *"I'm confused about what God wants me to do with the rest of my life. It's a fog to me. I just don't get it."* This lack of purpose can cause a woman to seek random activities to attempt to counteract boredom and her sometimes empty feeling of not having anything exciting to live for. This woman has difficulty understanding that our wise God has assigned her current tasks (including her spiritual growth) that are, presently, far more important than any big mission in the future. This woman is sometimes on the brink of losing hope because she has trouble understanding how the day-to-day grind matters in the broader scheme of fulfilling her purpose.

Why do you think this best describes you? Up til now (50)
I've always said wonder what I will be when I grow up! I think now (50 IAM + no clue.

☐ **The Guilty Woman** says, *"I understand what I'm supposed to do because I have heard God's call. There is no doubt in my mind as to my assignment, but I am having a great deal of difficulty focusing on it, getting organized around it, and not being afraid of it."* This woman is attempting to work on her current life purposes, but she gets sidetracked by life issues and fear. She needs some mentors, role models, and accountability partners to encourage her. She often finds herself loaded down with guilt over her nonperformance.

Why do you think this best describes you? _____

_____

☐ **The Stressed Woman** says, *"I am already doing what I was called to do; however, (and it's a big however) the rest of my world is somewhat out of balance or alignment. Actually, I have little time to breathe, and this is no way to live."* This woman has clarity of vision about her life purposes, but she has a gaping hole in her personal and/or family life that may be robbing her of gratitude and keeping her from soaring. Stress, dissatisfaction, and floundering relationships gnaw at her.

Why do you think this best describes you? _____

_____

☐ **The Grateful Woman** says, *"Thank you, Lord, that right now, things seem somewhat balanced and your vision for my life appears much clearer than before. Let me live in humble thankfulness for your gracious kindness toward me today. Brace me to deal with tomorrow's headaches tomorrow."* This woman is counting her blessings for her present season of life. She is on-track with her life purposes, without having derailed her relationships.

Why do you think this best describes you? _____

_____

(Be creative and fill in your own description below.)

☐ **The** _____ **Woman** says, _____

_____

_____

_____

_____

_____

_____

_____

Why do you think this best describes you? _____

_____

Whether you have no clue as to what your contribution will be, are confused about an organizational framework, are in short supply of personal and family balance, are enjoying a few moments of harmony, or have other specific feelings, you may be looking for some suggestion about how to achieve more concrete results.

Conversation Starters about the Self-Assessment for Purpose:

- Which of the five boxes did you mark? Why?
- Were you surprised, perhaps even saddened, by this self-assessment? Discuss your reaction with your Purpose Partner.

TODAY'S THIRD TOPIC: RELATIONSHIPS

Topic Three is dedicated to identifying people who have made a positive impact on your life. Your most treasured adult relationships might include your parents, siblings, fiancé, spouse, grown children, cousins, classmates, ministry leaders, coworkers, jogging partners, sailing buddies, or neighbors. They may be your best friends, mentors, accountability partners, role models, or heroes. Get ready to brag about them to your Purpose Partner. By thinking about how precious these people have been to you, you will be reminded that God designed you to enjoy the relationships he has provided. Not only are they essential for your spiritual growth, but they are his gift of loving kindness to you, as he works out his purposes for your life.

Think about what others have taught you, modeled for you, or given to you emotionally or spiritually. Ask yourself: What is it about a particular person that I absolutely love? Is it his or her loyalty, generosity, spontaneity, spirituality, hopefulness, tolerance, or courage? What is it about that person that drew us together and keeps us committed to one another? Is it his or her wisdom or unconditional love for me? Is what attracts me his or her creativity, wit, faithfulness, or stick-to-it-iveness? Is the person prayerful, teachable, analytical, brilliant, or caring? Does he or she listen well, pose good questions, or affirm me? Is it that I feel safe with that person and can talk about anything for hours? Do I most enjoy the laughter in our conversations, projects, or outings together?

Think about who has had a serious, healthy impact on your life. Jot down any names that come to mind in the following categories. You may have more than two names in any given section, but it is not necessary to fill in all the blanks. Make a notation about how the person's life impacted yours.

TREASURED RELATIONSHIPS

Best Friend: *One who sticks by you and loves you unconditionally.* Whose friendship have you cherished more than any other? With whom do you have a sweet history? Who understands you when nobody else does? Is it your husband or boyfriend, a ministry partner or neighbor?

Who? _Robin_ Why? _Unconditionally everything_

Who? _TaTa - Brenda_ Why? _dependable / encouraging_

Mentor: *A wise and trusted counselor or teacher.* Has that been a boss, financial counselor, grandparent, or church friend?

Who? _Robin_ Why? _always encouraging- subtle_

Who? _3rd Grade teacher_ Why? _- brought me to the Lord_

Accountability Partner: *A person who holds you responsible for your goals, roles, finances, or spiritual growth.* Who do you think of first? A lifelong friend, a sibling, or a woman in your Bible study?

Who? _Robin_ Why? _accountable for Growth in God_

Who? _Tate_ Why? _she always ask why w/questions_

Role Model: *Someone you look up to.* Does your pastor come to mind? Or perhaps your mom or a high school teacher?

Who? _Great Grandma_ Why? _- Peaceful, laughter, beliefs_

Who? _Robin_ Why? _being a Godly wife_

Modern-day or Historical Hero: *A person of courage; one who takes risks.* What about the late actor Christopher Reeve? Was he a more courageous Superman in your eyes after the horseback riding accident that left him paralyzed for nine years? What about someone you've read about in a history book or biography: Eleanor Roosevelt, Florence Nightingale, Winston Churchill, or others?

Who? _Lisa Paterson_ Why? _Christian wife, Loving mother_

Who? _Lee Ann Joye_ Why? _for her compassion, love, a zest for the right life._

Conversation Starters about Relationships:

- What names and reasons did you jot down?

- What memories did those names and notations stir up?

- In general, what do you or your Purpose Partner hear yourself saying about your relationships? Does it seem like you have too few, too many, the wrong kind, or a great blend of different types of relationships to move you toward God's purposes for your life? As the book of Ecclesiastes tells us, a cord of three strands (strong relationships) is not easily broken.

OPTIONAL CONVERSATION ENHANCER

CHERISHING YOUR BEST FRIEND

Friends love through all kinds of weather,
and families stick together in all kinds of trouble.
(PROVERBS 17:17, MSG)

Kay Marshall Strom is a speaker and author of more than thirty books on topics including blended families, caring for the dying, adoptions, and wife abuse. A passionate advocate for Christians around the world who are persecuted for their faith, she travels the globe to become personally acquainted with these men and women so she can bring their stories to Christians in America. And Kay has the dearest kind of friend, one who sticks by her through everything!

Together, Kay and her dearest friend, Gerda, have shared the best and the worst of times. Gerda was with Kay throughout the long terminal illness of Kay's first husband. In time, when Kay married Dan, Gerda was Kay's woman of honor. And, after a serious accident for Gerda, Kay showered her with countless expressions of practical, long-term love. Kay says, "Best friends don't always say what we want to hear, but they point us to God's Word and say what needs to be said. At least, that's what Gerda does for me."

Worth Chatting About: Elizabeth, the mother of John the Baptist, had a best friend in her cousin, Mary, the mother of Jesus (Luke 1:39–45). How happy would you be to see a cousin or best friend drop by for an unannounced, extended stay in your home?

TODAY'S FOURTH TOPIC: CHARACTERISTICS

One of the greatest gifts you can give yourself and your Purpose Partner is to remind each other of this truth: Good character can *move you toward* experiencing God's best in your lives, and character faults can *hold you back from* enjoying all the goodness that life has to offer. Of course, God can use you regardless of your character, but it's wisest to cooperate with him in this area.

For this exercise, which continues on pages 32–33, "Characteristics" is loosely defined to include character strengths as well as character flaws, good and bad habits, drives, and personality types. Check any characteristics that apply to you or write your answer.

CHARACTERISTICS

Character Strengths:

☒ Affectionate   ☒ Loving

☐ Authentic   ☒ Nurturing

☒ Compassionate   ☐ Observant

☐ Discerning   ☒ Persistent

☒ Encouraging   ☐ Reasonable

☐ Flexible   ☒ Reliable

☒ Friendly   ☒ Responsible

☒ Funny   ☒ Trustworthy

☒ Honest   ☐ Vulnerable

☒ Hopeful

☐ Humble   ☐ Other: _____

☐ Inspirational   ☐ Other: _____

☒ Intuitive   ☐ Other: _____

☒ Joyful

Character Flaws:

☒ Aggressive
☐ Angry all the time
☐ Ambitious to a fault
☐ Bitter
☒ Codependent
☐ Controlling
☒ Impatient
☐ Intimidating
☒ Intolerant
☐ Irresponsible

☐ Jealous
☒ Perfectionistic
☐ Prideful
☐ Rude
☐ Self-righteous
☐ Unfair
☐ Unkind
☐ Unreliable

☐ Other: _____

☐ Other: _____

Good Habits:

☐ Admitting mistakes
☐ Being punctual
☒ Establishing traditions
☐ Forgiving others
☐ Offering a smile

☒ Saying "I'm sorry"
☒ Serving behind the scenes
☒ Thanking or affirming people

☐ Other: _____

☐ Other: _____

Bad Habits:

☐ Apologizing all the time
☒ Being highly self-critical
☐ Blindsiding people to throw them off balance
☐ Enjoying the payoff of being a victim
☒ Exploding with a temper fit to get my way

☒ Finishing people's sentences
☐ Giving in to stress-induced insomnia
☒ Having trouble with male authority figures
☐ Making excuses for someone

☐ Other: _____

☐ Other: _____

What Drives Me?
- [ ] A challenge
- [ ] Changed lives
- [x] Commitment to a promise
- [x] Deadlines
- [x] God's will
- [ ] Power
- [ ] Purpose in life
- [ ] Recognition
- [x] Results
- [ ] Money
- [ ] Other: _____
- [ ] Other: _____

Personality Type:
- [x] Extrovert, who gets her energy from people
- [ ] Introvert, who gets her energy from being alone

Conversation Starter about Characteristics:
- What characteristics did you check or write, and why?

ANGER: A CHARACTERISTIC PREVALENT TODAY IN WOMEN

What do you get angry about? What pushes your button? Broken promises, lack of respect, wasted time, or unfair decisions? What makes your blood boil? Selfishness, poor excuses, unnecessary meetings, or animal cruelty? What sets off an anger-alarm inside your brain? Is it repeated mistakes, lack of pre-paredness, lack of control, losing things, change of plans, gaining weight, or people's tardiness? When do you find yourself losing it? Is it only when you've been lied to or cheated or manipulated?

If any of these things get to you, you're in good company with most women. Anger is a normal part of daily life, but what you choose to do with your anger can be helpful or hurtful to yourself and others. Clarity today about why, how often, or with whom you get angry will give you insight about your character. In turn, that will help you prepare for future difficult assignments that God may need you to tackle anger-free.

ANGRY?

"In your anger do not sin":
Do not let the sun go down while you are still angry.
(EPHESIANS 4:26)

Julie Ann Barnhill, author of such books as *She's Gonna Blow!* is a thought-provoking speaker who uses humor to make audiences "fasten their seatbelts." Her hilarious delivery and authentic confessions have made her a popular media guest and keynote speaker nationwide. Julie believes in the preposterous grace of God that is able to cover all her sins, hang-ups, mistakes, and frustrations. She voices the struggles that women are often afraid to admit out loud and lets them know this one truth: *You are not alone. Ever.*

She says that she had to finally admit that she was a "mess of magnificent proportions" as far as day-to-day parenting issues were concerned and that only God could change her angry heart and rebellious spirit. At last she chose to live life as it is—a journey of highs and lows, successes and failures—all to God's glory. She says, "No matter what you have said in anger, thought in anger, or acted out in anger, you have never fallen beyond the reach of God's grace and the hope of lasting change."

Worth Chatting About: In what way has a character fault, such as anger, jealousy, laziness, or pride, been a problem for you?

anger-John

Searching Scripture Together for Wisdom about Anger: Read Genesis 27:41 about a major anger problem. Esau hated his brother Jacob so much (because of Jacob's manipulation in securing their father's blessing) that he intended to kill him. **Something to Talk About:** Share whether a character issue you have battled (perhaps anger, prejudice, impatience, ambition, or perfectionism) has ever escalated out of control.

So . . . What Are Your Final Thoughts about Characteristics?

- Has this broad category about characteristics given you some insights into what God is specifically asking you to notice about yourself and the way you do life? Discuss with your Purpose Partner what segments of this exercise encouraged you or saddened you and why you think you reacted as you did.

- If God were sitting in the room physically with you today, what characteristic might he say is blessing or interfering with your ability to live the best life possible?

Wrapping Up

PRAYER LOG:

While this workbook focuses on your conversations with your Purpose Partner, it will lack true power without regular conversations with the Giver of purpose, your heavenly Father—both on your own and together. Before you end your time today, take a few minutes to share prayer requests and praises with each other, using the Prayer Log that begins on page 140. Then use the closing prayer provided here, supplementing as desired. For your daily, private prayers regarding any requests, feel free to use the prayer on page 139.

CLOSE YOUR TIME TOGETHER IN CONVERSATION WITH GOD:

Dear God, help us honor our Purpose Partner Commitment to one another. We know that it will only be through your grace that we work together as a great team to better understand your will. Thank you for your insights through the Self-Assessment about Purpose, as well as our conversation today about characteristics, knowing that you are well aware of our best and worst ones.

Alan Jackson —

And, dear Lord, we pray that we will enjoy a lifetime of healthy, loving relationships. Bless those you have stationed along the way in our lives as best friends, mentors, accountability partners, role models, and heroes. Never let us be lone rangers. You have taught us that friends love through all kinds of weather and that families stick together in all kinds of trouble. Teach our friends how to give us the support and unconditional love we need, so we will be encouraged to do whatever you ask of us. Help us be an intentional friend to others as well. In Jesus' name, we pray. Amen.

BEFORE YOUR NEXT CONVERSATION:

- Read the chapter and complete the exercises for Conversation #2.
- Pray diligently for your Purpose Partner's prayer requests, as well as your own. Spend time throughout the week praising God for who he is and for all he has done for both of you. Ask specifically for him to shed light on your next conversation, which will be about some of the basic indicators of your current life purposes and the tools useful in fulfilling them.

AGREEING ABOUT THE BASICS OF YOUR PURPOSES

Open Your Time Together in Conversation with God: *Dear God, today we ask for your guidance in the areas of our roles, core values and beliefs, spiritual habits, and strengths. We know that you care deeply about the healthy development of these things in our lives, and so we ask that you will be specific in your instructions and next steps. In Jesus' name, we pray. Amen.*

Just for Fun: Share about a time you got in trouble for something—as a child, teen, or adult. Walking into fence - careye. I was responsible for her after school, walking home.

TODAY'S FIRST TOPIC: ROLES

Are your life roles balanced or out of whack? What's the most challenging role in your life these days? What makes it hard for you to get out of bed each morning, knowing that you have to face it again? Are you the parent of a rebellious teen, employee of a hard-to-please boss, daughter of a parent with Alzheimer's, sometime-driver in an unreliable carpool, or single mother of four active children? (wife to a controlling, undisciplined husband

It seems as if there is always something that keeps us off balance, tempting us to run off to a remote island for a long vacation. Have you just been given another role to fulfill? Financial advisor to a newlywed couple, comforter to someone who got fired, justice-fighter for a cause, teacher of dyslexic children, or spiritual director for your best friend? Let each tough role bring you closer to God, as you learn to rely on his power and faithfulness to fulfill his purposes for your life today. He will be there to guide you every step of the way.

Check any roles that currently apply to you or write your answer. (If you also want to put an asterisk behind any roles you previously have had, that might be an interesting exercise too, but you won't be asked any further questions about those.)

ROLES AND MORE ROLES

- ☐ Accountability partner
- ☑ Aunt
- ☑ Best friend
- ☐ Boss
- ☐ Career woman
- ☐ Caregiver
- ☐ Church member
- ☐ Coach
- ☐ Community volunteer
- ☐ Confidante
- ☐ Cook
- ☑ Daughter
- ☐ Daughter of the King
- ☐ Employee
- ☐ Entrepreneur
- ☐ Ex-wife
- ☐ Financial manager
- ☐ Girlfriend
- ☐ Grandmother
- ☑ Household engineer
- ☐ Kids' taxi driver

- ☐ Lay minister
- ☐ Licensed minister
- ☐ Mentor
- ☑ Mother
- ☐ Mother-in-law
- ☑ Neighbor
- ☐ Pastor's wife
- ☐ Protégé
- ☑ Purpose Partner
- ☐ Roommate
- ☐ Single mother
- ☑ Sister
- ☐ Student
- ☑ Tutor (teacher)
- ☑ Wife
- ☐ World traveler

- ☐ Other: _____
- ☐ Other: _____
- ☐ Other: _____

Conversation Starters about Your Roles:

- Talk about the wide variety of roles you have. How does your list bring new meaning to the term *multitasking*?

- What is your greatest challenge in maintaining your balance as you live out your many roles?

BALANCING SOME ROLES AND WALKING AWAY FROM SOME OTHERS

Be very careful, then, how you live—not as unwise but as wise.
(EPHESIANS 5:15)

Carla Barnhill is a married mother of three who works from her home as Senior Editor of *Christian Parenting Today* magazine and author of *The Myth of the Perfect Mother*. She says she fell into writing and editing by a sheer act of God's grace, but enjoys the privilege of using her faith in her work and counts it a genuine blessing to seek God alongside her readers.

Carla's greatest personal challenge is juggling the competing demands for her time and attention. Her husband, children, extended family, church, friends, home, and career all call for her best efforts, and without fail, something always slips. She says that she used to have a strong tendency to grab on to opportunities because they seemed like the right thing to do at the time, but she almost always regretted overextending herself. She's now learning to differentiate between God's best for her life and doors of opportunity she can choose to close. She adds, "There is no role too challenging for you when you hold the hand of God. God has proved to be faithful since the beginning of time. And, God gives good advice about saying no to opportunities that could prevent you from completing the work God gave you to do."

Worth Chatting About: What door of opportunity do you think you should close? Why?

Searching Scripture Together for Wisdom about Roles: Read Exodus 2:1–10 and Hebrews 11:23 about the difficult role Moses' parents had. They had to hide Moses, their infant, in a papyrus basket among the reeds along the bank of the Nile to prevent him from being killed. God has assigned you some challenging roles too. **Something to Talk About:** Think about one of the most difficult roles you have ever had. Share how you navigated (or are navigating) your way through the tough assignment.

So . . . What Are Your Final Thoughts about Roles?

- Discuss together any insights into what God is accomplishing in your life through your roles or where you need his guidance. As iron sharpens iron, challenge one another to believe that God, in his sovereignty, already knows precisely what he wants to achieve, eternally, in your life and the life of each person he sends your way.

TODAY'S SECOND TOPIC: CORE VALUES AND BELIEFS

Roles are usually fairly obvious; they fill our waking hours (and sometimes what should be our sleeping hours!). Core values and beliefs are less obvious, and less discussed, but certainly no less important. If roles are the ship, core values and beliefs are what steer the ship. They are what's bigger than we are, the unwritten guidelines we live by, the things we hold dearest.

The next two exercises will help you bring these values and beliefs to the surface so that you can inspect them more carefully and better understand how they support your daily and long-term purposes. On pages 41–42 check any core values and beliefs that apply to you or write your answer.

WHAT TEN THINGS DO I VALUE MOST?

- ☑ A reward in heaven
- ☑ Achieving goals and dreams
- ☑ Appearance(s)
- ☑ Being fulfilled
- ☐ Being right
- ☐ Christlike service
- ☑ Commitment
- ☐ Control
- ☐ Duty
- ☐ Fame
- ☑ Family
- ☑ Friendships
- ☑ Health
- ☑ Independence
- ☐ Innovation
- ☐ Intellectual pursuits
- ☐ Money
- ☐ Perfection
- ☐ Personal possessions
- ☐ Physical challenges

- ☑ Pleasant environment
- ☐ Popularity
- ☐ Power
- ☐ Prestige
- ☐ Recognition
- ☑ Relationships
- ☑ Relationship with Jesus
- ☑ Reputation
- ☑ Safety
- ☑ Schedules
- ☐ Success
- ☐ Teamwork
- ☐ To-do lists
- ☑ Travel
- ☐ Wealth
- ☐ Other: _____
- ☐ Other: _____
- ☐ Other: _____

My Beliefs

As the old saying goes regarding beliefs: "If you don't know what you stand for, you're likely to fall for anything." Fill in the six blanks below with statements such as, "I believe in . . ."

Affirmative Action

Asking for forgiveness

Asking for what I want

The Bible

The Bill of Rights

Bringing glory to God

Civil rights

Dignity for all people

Doing the best I can

Forgiving others

Giving more than I expect to receive

God, Jesus, and the Holy Spirit

Having a positive attitude

Listening well

Never giving up

Not fretting that I will fail

People helping people

Philanthropy

Prayer in school

Putting God first

Showing empathy, trust, and honesty

The Ten Commandments

Trying to outgive God

The unity of my family

Using the gifts God gave me

Working hard

- _____
- _____
- _____
- _____
- _____
- _____

Conversation Starters about Your Core Values and Beliefs:

• What values and beliefs do you hold most dear?

• Talk about something you once valued or once believed that you don't hold as valuable or believable anymore.

• Your core values and beliefs may speak volumes about your life purposes. Could any of your values or beliefs possibly hold a clue to what God wants you to do with your life now or in the future? Don't force any answers. Just pose the question and see if God reveals anything today.

TODAY'S THIRD TOPIC: SPIRITUAL HABITS

Spiritual habits are intended to make you more like Christ, to help you become holy. A great side benefit, though, is that they also help you hear from God about his will for your life. Some of the habits, disciplines, or methods people use to hear God's will include extended times of prayerful solitude, journaling, reading Scripture, or listening to worship music. Some report that God speaks audibly, while others say he allows his Holy Spirit to impress his thoughts on them.

Do you feel like you have a direct line to God, or do you marvel when others say things like: "God told me . . ."? Because there is no one correct way to communicate with God and hear his voice, you may have success in one of these ways: asking him questions and then listening for his answers; fasting; living a lifestyle of daily worship in all you do; or confessing and repenting of your sins. You may hear God most clearly when you surrender something specific to him; forgive yourself or someone else; or seek intimacy with him, not just knowledge. Slow down today and allow some silence in your life, as you reflect on the disciplines you have or would like to develop. On the next page check those spiritual habits that you practice regularly or write your answer. Put an asterisk by those you have checked or written that particularly help you hear God's voice.

SPIRITUAL HABITS

- ☐ Bible reading
- ☐ Bible study
- ☐ Confession
- ☐ Conversing with God all day long
- ☐ Extended times of solitude
- ☐ Fasting
- ☐ Forgiveness
- ☐ Journaling
- ☐ Keeping the Sabbath
- ☐ Prayer
- ☐ Praying the names of God
- ☐ Purity

- ☐ Quiet time
- ☐ Repentance
- ☐ Scripture meditation
- ☐ Scripture memorization
- ☐ Silence
- ☐ Singing praises to God
- ☐ Surrender
- ☐ Tithing
- ☐ Worship
- ☐ Other: _____
- ☐ Other: _____

Conversation Starters about Your Spiritual Habits:

- Talk about the spiritual habits you checked or wrote. Share an example of a good or bad experience you had with one of them.

- Which habits did you asterisk? Why do you feel they particularly help you hear God's voice?

- Is there something you or your Purpose Partner said about spiritual habits that needs to be unpacked further or a thought that is weighing on your heart that you'd like to discuss? Talk about where you are succeeding or may want more direction in regard to the development of spiritual disciplines in your life.

THE SPIRITUAL HABIT OF LISTENING FOR GOD'S DIRECTION

"Call to Me [God] and I will answer you, and I will tell you great and mighty things, which you do not know."
(JEREMIAH 33:3, NASB)

Carol Bauer, in partnership with her husband, Gary, and American Values, the pro-family, public policy group, seeks to strengthen American families based on Judeo-Christian principles. She writes a monthly *Prayer Alert* newsletter from Washington, D.C., that goes out to tens of thousands of readers. Her strong faith and being a mother of three (ages eighteen to twenty-seven) have prepared her as a mentor for moms of preschoolers, as well as a small group leader for moms of teenagers. She encourages mothers to apply godly principles to their role of raising children and is blessed when they are real enough with each other to chuckle, "Your kids do that too?" or to exclaim, "I thought I was the only one facing that!" Carol loves to call on God in all circumstances, and she hungers to learn new things he wants to teach her.

Carol says that she attempts to discern God's will in this way: "If I faithfully read his Word, offer praises to him, seek his insights, pour out my fears, questions, and anger to him . . . and then listen to his leading, advice, and encouragement, I discover his desire for my life. That's actually the easy part. The hard part is that, then, I must obey." She adds, "To be able to discern God's will requires us to stay as close to our Savior as we do to our dearest friend."

Worth Chatting About: If you heard God's will today for your life, would you obey it?

TODAY'S FOURTH TOPIC: STRENGTHS

All believers have talents, skills, abilities, and spiritual gifts. Sometimes we readily (and hopefully, humbly!) acknowledge these strengths in ourselves. But other times we are guilty of thinking we're not good or gifted at anything. In either case, take this opportunity to honestly assess your strengths. Check all items that apply to you or write your answer. And thank God for how he has equipped you to serve him in our world in a specific way.

MY INCREDIBLE STRENGTHS

Talents, Skills, and Abilities:

Strengths can include your talents, resume-type skills, and abilities.

- ☐ Accounting
- ☐ Acting
- ☐ Counseling
- ☐ Court reporting
- ☐ Drawing
- ☐ Graphic design
- ☐ Interior decorating
- ☐ Languages
- ☐ Marketing
- ☐ Organizing
- ☐ Painting
- ☐ Reading blueprints
- ☐ Sculpting
- ☐ Selling

- ☐ Shorthand
- ☐ Singing
- ☐ Supervising others
- ☐ Technology
- ☐ Thinking clearly under pressure
- ☐ Typing
- ☐ Writing fiction
- ☐ Writing poetry

- ☐ Other: _____
- ☐ Other: _____
- ☐ Other: _____

Spiritual Giftedness:

Spiritual gifts are those strengths given by the Holy Spirit to be specifically used in building the kingdom of God. You may have been born with them or have been given them for a season of service. (For more information on this topic, see *Praying for Purpose for Women*, pages 214–215. Included there are several excellent resources.)

- ☐ Administration
- ☐ Apostle
- ☐ Celibacy
- ☐ Discernment
- ☐ Encouragement
- ☐ Evangelism
- ☐ Faith
- ☐ Giving
- ☐ Healing
- ☐ Helps
- ☐ Hospitality
- ☐ Intercessory praying

- ☐ Knowledge and wisdom
- ☐ Leadership
- ☐ Mercy
- ☐ Missionary
- ☐ Prophecy
- ☐ Service
- ☐ Shepherd/pastor
- ☐ Teaching
- ☐ Voluntary poverty
- ☐ Wisdom

- ☐ Other: _____

Conversation Starters about Strengths:

• What talents, skills, and abilities or spiritual gifts did you check or write?

• Give a specifc example when one of these strengths was evident in your life.

• What feelings do you have about your particular strengths or perceived lack thereof?

• What do you think you are supposed to do with your strengths or about your lack of them?

Wrapping Up

PRAYER LOG:

Update your Prayer Log on page 140 as you share prayer requests and praise reports.

CLOSE YOUR TIME TOGETHER IN CONVERSATION WITH GOD:

Dear God, thank you for being part of our conversation today. We pray that we will daily praise you for who you are and that we will ask for your will to be done through us to your glory. Whatever it is that you have planned for us on any particular day, show us the way we should go. Thank you for the current roles you have assigned us and help us to find balance in them. We want to follow your promptings about what to value and what to believe. We want to practice spiritual habits that help us grow up into Christlikeness and a maturity in our faith. And we ask that you increase our strengths, especially our spiritual giftedness, so we can accomplish more for you. In Jesus' name, we pray. Amen.

Before Your Next Conversation:

- Read the chapter and complete the exercises for Conversation #3.
- Think about how you and your Purpose Partner will take a day off together to enjoy each other's company during Conversation #7, *Taking a Laughter Break*. Depending on your budget, you may want to go hiking or window shopping; make a dessert or a craft; go to brunch or high tea; have a picnic or game night; catch a movie or musical; watch family videos or a documentary; visit a museum or amusement park; take a drive or a swim; go to a seminar or sports event; get a manicure or a makeover; or check out each other's hobbies. Plan on finalizing the details during Conversation #6.
- Pray diligently for your Purpose Partner's prayer requests, as well as your own. Spend time throughout the week praising God for who he is and for all he has done for both of you. Prepare your heart in prayer for your next conversation, so you can unearth the things that are acting as blockades to your life purposes.

Conversation #3

UNEARTHING BLOCKADES TO YOUR PURPOSES

Open Your Time Together in Conversation with God: *Dear God, today we ask for your answers in the areas of our motives, fear, grief, and mistaken thinking. We know that you are the only one who can open our eyes and help us see the truth about how these things affect our ability to follow your lead daily. We trust that you will guide us in a specific way today. In Jesus' name, we pray. Amen.*

Just for Fun: Share about one of your pet peeves or family traditions.

TODAY'S FIRST TOPIC: MOTIVES

Masks and costumes disguise people. They cover up what's real, creating pretense or a false outward show. When donned for a play or a party, the illusion is all in fun. But when appearances are purposefully deceitful in everyday life, the result is much more serious. Are there any pretenses that you maintain? Do you, for example, tend to hide your true motives? Do you wear fake smiles, like some soldiers wear camouflage makeup? What "make-nice" efforts are you displaying, when just below the surface, your reasons for doing something are not pretty at all?

Today, begin to live a more authentic life by more thoroughly understanding your motives, your reasons for doing things. This insight will help you learn to be more authentic with God when he calls on you to do something for him. In the following exercise, you will see a question: **Am I _____ in order to _____?** Acquaint yourself with the list of possible answers, and then fill in the blanks with the words closest to your own personal experiences.

MY IMPURE AND PURE MOTIVES

Impure Motives:

Am I _____

<small>(Fill in the blank with a **positive or negative action from your own life,** like one of these below)</small>

- asking for prayer
- attending an event
- cheating
- counseling a friend
- doing a kind deed
- embarrassing someone
- encouraging a person

- fasting
- giving an expensive gift
- giving a speech
- gossiping
- judging someone
- lying
- making a donation

- making amends
- praying
- seeking forgiveness
- sending a card
- serving on a committee
- stealing
- tithing

in order to _____?

<small>(Fill in the blank with an **impure motive from your own life,** like one of these below.)</small>

- be famous, powerful, or wealthy
- be in the in-crowd
- be puffed up with knowledge
- build my reputation
- cause a thrill
- cause someone's indebtedness to me
- control someone

- ease my shame or guilt
- feel good about what I did
- feel some drama, theatrics, or passion
- fulfill my obligation or duty
- get recognition, attention, affirmation, or a reward
- get pity or sympathy
- get revenge

- gossip
- impress someone
- increase my status
- manipulate a response
- make people like me
- mask my pain, boredom, jealousy, or loneliness
- reduce embarrassment
- relieve my anger
- rub shoulders with someone famous
- satisfy my curiosity
- secure bragging rights
- show off my talent, beauty, or knowledge
- stir up trouble
- take advantage of people's emotions or wallets

Pure Motives:

Am I _____

(Fill in the blank with a **positive or negative action from your own life.** Use the list from the Impure Motives question to trigger ideas.)

in order to _____?

(Fill in the blank with a **pure motive from your own life**, like one of these below.)

- give glory to God
- represent Jesus to someone
- spread the good news of the gospel

Conversation Starters about Motives:

- What answers did you fill in?
- In what way did your answers surprise you?
- Knowing what you now know about your motives, discuss together where you most need God's power. Ask your Purpose Partner if she has any insights about her own motives that might help you.

UNCOVERING AN UGLY MOTIVE

*The LORD searches every heart and understands
every motive behind the thoughts.*
(1 CHRONICLES 28:9)

Quin Sherrer has written or coauthored twenty-four books, among them *Prayers from a Grandma's Heart*, *Miracles Happen When You Pray*, and *God Be with Us*. Through her speaking and more than three hundred radio and television appearances, she desires to encourage women with practical, biblical, and sometimes humorous insights.

Before Quin began her writing ministry, God revealed to her an ugly motive in her heart that took root when she was just twelve years old. Angry at her father for leaving her mother to marry another woman, she continued to let her hatred grow as, in the following years, he refused to acknowledge major milestones in her life—her college graduation, wedding, and the birth of three children. Because he was ignoring and hurting her, she decided she would do likewise to him. When a sermon at last convinced her of her bitter and resentful attitude, she asked God to forgive her and chose to forgive her dad as well. God then seemed to drop a bucket of love in her heart for her dad and she began writing letters to him. Five years later he traveled to see her and eventually asked, "How could you love me after all I've done?" She gave him a big bear hug. Jesus had indeed changed her.

"When we are dealing with a wrong motive in our hearts," says Quin, "only God's Spirit can reshape us." A writing career and a restored relationship with her dad are the wonderful results of that reshaping in Quin's life.

Worth Chatting About: Think about someone you tend to treat poorly. What ugly motive in your heart causes you to disregard the value of that relationship (for example, anger, jealousy, revenge, feeling of superiority, or the need to control)?

Today's Second Topic: Fear

My favorite synonyms for fear are *apprehension* and *dread*, rather than *horror* or *terror*. To me, the first two describe the fear that we live with daily; the last two describe the fear that haunts women more rarely. Do you live with either type of fear? Does your fear feel manageable or out of control? Does it cause mental paralysis that makes you unreceptive to God's leading? The sentences below can be strong indicators of fear:

- What will others say if I pursue God's plan for my life?
- I can't do it; it's way too hard.
- I don't know where to begin.
- God couldn't possibly want *me* for that assignment!

It is difficult to break through the barrier of fear, so just be patient with yourself. God loves you and can use you even when you're afraid. In the exercise on this page and the next check any of fears that apply to you today or write your answer. Put an asterisk after any that used to apply.

Fears

☐ Abandonment
☐ Accidents
☐ Admitting a sin
☐ AIDS
☐ Bankruptcy
☐ Being alone
☐ Being attacked
☐ Being fired
☐ Being found out
☐ Being murdered
☐ Being seen as incompetent
☐ Breast cancer
☐ Bridges

☐ Chemical warfare
☐ Confrontation
☐ Criticism
☐ Disappointing someone
☐ Dying young
☐ Enclosed spaces
☐ Evangelism
☐ Failing an exam
☐ Fire
☐ Flood
☐ Flying
☐ Getting old and feeble
☐ Giving a speech

(continued)

- ☐ Going to the doctor
- ☐ Heights
- ☐ Jellyfish
- ☐ Joining a new ministry
- ☐ Joining a small group
- ☐ Losing my home
- ☐ Moral failure
- ☐ Not being productive
- ☐ Not having a purpose
- ☐ Rejection
- ☐ Ridicule

- ☐ Snakes
- ☐ Spiders
- ☐ Starting a new job
- ☐ Success
- ☐ Talking to a stranger
- ☐ Terrorism
- ☐ Other: _____
- ☐ Other: _____
- ☐ Other: _____

Conversation Starters about Fear:

- What fears did you check, write, and/or asterisk?

- Select several fears to talk about more extensively.

- What do you think God is trying to impress on you about your fears? Is he challenging you to move away from one of them or congratulating you for having already done so?

- Let your Purpose Partner play devil's advocate today, asking you how your "fear of a fear" might keep you from God's best.

TODAY'S THIRD TOPIC: GRIEF

Grief finds us in many ways. Your grief may have been caused because your teenager ran away; a friend deceived you; you were treated unfairly at work; or a natural disaster destroyed your home. You may have had to struggle with chronic fatigue syndrome, bankruptcy, a job layoff, the threat of terminal illness, a parent's death, or your husband's admission of homosexuality. You may have endured date rape, depression, or public humiliation.

When life tragedies break you, God will gladly step in to use your brokenness to shape and perfect you—if you let him. Can you see how faithfully God has been maturing you spiritually through your most difficult life experiences? Reflect on what your brokenness has taught you. Are you more humble, grateful, sensitive, compassionate, or prayerful because of what you have lived through? Have you learned to be more patient, encouraging, gentle, generous, forgiving, or dependent on God? It's helpful to acknowledge how you have suffered and whether you surrendered the hurt to God for him to use to complete his work on earth.

For the exercise on page 58, let's define *grief* as any sadness, loss, pain, failure, or sorrow you have had to deal with, whether that was a crisis in your own life or in the life of your spouse, child, or dearest friend. If a tragedy changed you forever, you will be asked to check it. Follow the rest of the instructions on the top of the Grief Map.

You may have had numerous painful experiences in your life, or you may have had relatively little sorrow. For some women, this chart is a denial buster. After looking at all the items they marked, they say, "I never realized I had been through so much." It is not uncommon, for example, for a woman to check over half of the seventy-two items.

The most important aspect of this exercise, though, is *not* how many items you check but to honestly answer the question that follows the chart, "What wounds are still open?" You see, the point is this: Have you healed enough to move on? If you haven't, you need to focus on the process of healing so you can, eventually, move on.

The circumstances of your past can help you find purpose and fulfillment in your life as you befriend someone who is experiencing a crisis that you have already lived through. Put another way, your grief is meant to be recycled into something useful that blesses the life of another, as soon as you're able.

GRIEF MAP

1. Check any words related to your past or present pain/grief.
2. Put an "H" for "Healed" next to those checkmarked experiences you feel you have worked through.
3. Put an asterisk by your worst pain or ache.

☐ Abuse
☐ Accident
☐ Adoption
☐ Affair
☐ AIDS
☐ Alcohol-related event
☐ Anorexia
☐ Appearance
☐ Bankruptcy
☐ Battering
☐ Betrayed
☐ Blindness
☐ Broken dream
☐ Bulimia
☐ Burglarized
☐ Business failure
☐ Cancer
☐ Carjacking
☐ Deafness
☐ Death
☐ Death of an unsaved friend
☐ Depression
☐ Discrimination
☐ Disease
☐ Disowned

☐ Divorce
☐ Drug-related issue
☐ Dying
☐ Empty nest
☐ Fired
☐ Flasher
☐ Gang-related situation
☐ Gunshot
☐ Handicap
☐ Harassment
☐ Heart attack
☐ Hijacking
☐ Illness
☐ Incest
☐ Infertility
☐ Injury
☐ Insomnia
☐ Jail term
☐ Jilted
☐ Laid off
☐ Loss of friendship
☐ Loss of home
☐ Loss of limb
☐ Military separation
☐ Miscarriage

☐ Money problems
☐ Natural disaster
☐ Panic attacks
☐ Probate
☐ Rape
☐ Rebellious child
☐ Relocation
☐ Retardation
☐ Retirement
☐ School dropout
☐ Separation
☐ Sexual problems
☐ Stalked
☐ Stillborn child
☐ Stroke
☐ Suicide
☐ Surgery
☐ Teen runaway
☐ Torn family
☐ Unemployment
☐ Unwanted pregnancy
☐ Weight-related circumstance
☐ _____
☐ _____
☐ _____

> What wounds are still open? _____
> _____
> _____

Conversation Starters about Grief:

- What issues did you check, write, mark with an "H," and/or asterisk?

- How did you answer the question, "What wounds are still open?"

- What questions or thoughts do you have about how God might want to recycle your grief?

- How are you doing with this topic? Let your Purpose Partner help you process your feelings.

Optional Conversation Enhancer

WHEN YOUR HEART BREAKS INTO MANY PIECES

Praise be to the God and Father of our Lord Jesus Christ,
the Father of compassion and the God of all comfort,
who comforts us in all our troubles, so that we can comfort those
in any trouble with the comfort we ourselves have received from God.
(2 CORINTHIANS 1:3-4)

Karen Johnson is a licensed professional counselor, author, thirty-year teacher of the Bible, and television-radio personality. For fifteen years, she hosted and produced the daily, nationwide, call-in television program, *COPE*. During that time, she answered more than 50,000 calls from people all over America who needed advice.

But at the age of fifty-three, life collapsed on Karen. It was then that her husband of thirty years asked for a divorce; her widowed mother almost died

(Karen is an only child); her two dogs died; she lost her job, church, home, and friends; and she continued to deal with the fact that she had not been able to have children due to medical complications. All this forced her to completely start over. Broken, she hung on to Isaiah 54:5, "For your Maker is your husband—the LORD Almighty is his name." She says, "God asks each of us to become better, not bitter, no matter what happens to us!" Today she loves helping women (especially those over forty-five) make a difference in their world, no matter what their past or present circumstances.

Worth Chatting About: From what you have learned about brokenness over the years, what advice would you have given to Karen when she was hurting so badly?

Searching Scripture Together for Wisdom about Grief: Read Job 42:10–17. God allowed Satan to break Job's life in every aspect (family, health, wealth, reputation, and friendships), so that he, God, might be glorified by Job's testimony. God later made Job twice as prosperous as he was before as a reward for his faithfulness during the dark hours. **Something to Talk About:** Do you marvel at the extent of Job's brokenness and his increasing reliance on God? Talk about how you think you might have reacted in Job's situation.

So . . . What Are Your Final Thoughts about Grief?

• What have you or your Purpose Partner noticed about your grief: that you don't like to deal with it as it occurs? that you are constantly "waiting for the other shoe to drop"? or that you easily learn what it has to teach you? Talk freely about your reaction to grief in your life or in the lives of others.

TODAY'S FOURTH TOPIC: MISTAKEN THINKING

Mistaken thinking can creep into our lives unconsciously. It quite often happens, at an early age, that we are taught something born out of someone else's insecurity, prejudice, or ignorance. Be honest. What viewpoint have you internalized that you have tried to unlearn? Think about how mistaken thinking could interfere with what God asks you to be and do on earth. Check or write any that reflect what you learned—whether or not you still hold those ideas!

MISTAKEN THINKING

☐ Complete a task at any cost.
☐ Don't trust anyone.
☐ Don't trust men.
☐ God loves me, only if I'm productive.
☐ Good works will get me into heaven.
☐ I am an island.
☐ I can fix people.
☐ I can't.
☐ I can't please God, no matter what.
☐ I don't fit.
☐ I'm a survivor.
☐ I'm a bad person.
☐ I'm entitled!
☐ I'm not good enough.
☐ I'm stupid.
☐ I'm superwoman.
☐ I'm supposed to be a perfect mom.
☐ I'm ugly.

☐ I'm unworthy of love.
☐ I must overcompensate for my lack.
☐ I need to look out for #1!
☐ I need to save or rescue people.
☐ I shouldn't.
☐ I was born tired.
☐ I will get caught up on my to-do list.
☐ Manipulation works.
☐ My past will cripple my future.
☐ Never give up control.
☐ People are cruel.
☐ Self-esteem is based on good looks, riches, popularity, or power.
☐ The Bible is fiction.
☐ There are no absolutes.

☐ Other: _____

☐ Other: _____

Conversation Starters about Mistaken Thinking:

- Tell your Purpose Partner what you checked or wrote.

- Talk about whether you have ditched some or all of your previously-held mistaken thinking.

- Is there any one concept, in particular, that you need to disown right now so you can be freed to answer God's call on your life? If so, let your Purpose Partner help you take a good look at it today. Your goal is to laughingly say, "Isn't that ridiculous! I'm not going to buy into that any longer."

- Talk with your Purpose Partner about any feelings you are having about your mistaken thinking. Feelings might include anger at having been duped at an early age by someone you trusted, joy at having seen the light, or excitement about telling someone else what you have just discovered. Discuss how you think God feels about any insight you gained today.

Wrapping Up

Prayer Log:

Update your Prayer Log on page 140 as you share prayer requests and praise reports.

Close Your Time Together in Conversation with God:

Dear God, thank you for being part of our conversation today. How could we ever live without you? Move us away from those things that are blocking us from following your plan for our lives, especially our impure motives, fear, and grief. Today, we ask specifically for you, the Father of compassion, and the God of all comfort, who comforts us in all our troubles, to help us comfort those in any trouble with the comfort we ourselves have received from you. And help us disown our mistaken thinking that has been holding us back from your best in our lives. Move us toward living the life we were meant to live. In Jesus' name, we pray. Amen.

Before Your Next Conversation:

- Read the chapter and complete the exercises for Conversation #4.
- Pray diligently for your Purpose Partner's prayer requests, as well as your own. Spend time throughout the week praising God for who he is and for all he has done for both of you. Get yourself prayerfully ready to enjoy the fun side of your unique purpose in your next conversation.

Conversation #4

Enjoying the Fun Side of Your Unique Purpose

Open Your Time Together in Conversation with God: *Dear God, today we ask for your wise counsel in the areas of our inspiration, successes, miracles, and passions. Send your Holy Spirit to us as a Magnificent Counselor, who breathes honesty and clarity into our time together, so we might more fully magnify you with our lives. In Jesus' name, we pray. Amen.*

Just for Fun: Share something about your favorite restaurant, hotel, or car.

Today's First Topic: Inspiration

Understanding how you can invite inspiration into your life is critical to being able to go the distance in completing your life purposes. Some women become creative by recharging their batteries (resting), rewarding themselves, learning something new, exercising, or all of those. On pages 66–67 check any methods of inspiration that work for you or write your answer.

INSPIRATION

How do you *recharge your batteries or rest* during a long haul to ensure continued creativity? This is the art of using your downtime to help you regroup.

☐ Praying
☐ Gardening
☐ Having friends over for a barbecue
☐ Pondering philosophy in a hammock
☐ Reading by a fireplace
☐ Smelling roses
☐ Strolling along the beach
    with my spouse or boyfriend

☐ Taking naps
☐ Window shopping with a friend
    or family member

☐ Other: _____

☐ Other: _____

How do you *reward* yourself to invite inspiration? Don't write "ice cream"! Think of things that unlock the doors of creativity, not clog your system. Also, be careful to think of things that are true gifts to you, not methods of escape.

☐ Bubble bath
☐ Date night
☐ Family night
☐ Favorite CD
☐ Jazz concert
☐ Lunch at a sidewalk cafe
☐ Mystery movie
☐ Pat on the back

☐ Playtime with my grandchildren
☐ Shakespearean play

☐ Other: _____

☐ Other: _____

☐ Other: _____

☐ Other: _____

In what way do you try to *learn something new*? Do you learn best through a . . .

☐ Book/article
☐ Class/seminar
☐ Friend
☐ Hobby
☐ Sermon/song
☐ Time of observation

☐ Video/audio

☐ Other: _____

☐ Other: _____

☐ Other: _____

How do you *exercise*? What do you do to keep your blood circulating? Do you . . .

☐ Ballroom dance
☐ Bike
☐ Climb a Stair Master
☐ Jog
☐ Kayak
☐ Kickbox

☐ Play tennis
☐ Swim
☐ Take an aerobics class

☐ Other: _____
☐ Other: _____

Conversation Starters about Inspiration:

• What items did you check or write? Talk more about several of your favorite ways of inviting creativity into your life.

• Ask your Purpose Partner what she feels the main "takeaway" is from today's exercise in regard to fulfilling God's daily and long-term plans. Discuss your thoughts on the matter.

TODAY'S SECOND TOPIC: SUCCESSES

Successes in your life have shaped who you are, and they can act as great reminders of what you are capable of doing with God's help. Who knows? Some of your successes may be used to bless the kingdom in some way. Now is *not* the time to be shy with false humility about how you have succeeded in life, whether that's been recognized through awards or not. Now is the time to record the truth about your minor and major accomplishments. Whether something happened long ago or is a more current success, on the next page check any that apply to you or write your answer.

SUCCESSES IN MY LIFE

During my school years:

- ☐ Completed a 4H project
- ☐ Earned a diploma or college degree
- ☐ Had a role in a school production
- ☐ Held a class or club office
- ☐ Learned to play the piano
  or other instrument

- ☐ Made a sports team
- ☐ Maintained a high GPA
- ☐ Went on a mission trip
- ☐ Other: _____
- ☐ Other: _____

And later in life:

- ☐ Am a faithful, loving wife
- ☐ Am a trustworthy parent
- ☐ Bought my own home
  or decorated one
- ☐ Built a company or a boat or a team
- ☐ Cared for an invalid parent
- ☐ Delivered an important speech well
- ☐ Discipled a new believer
- ☐ Held a political office
- ☐ Led someone to the Lord

- ☐ Made a profit for my company
- ☐ Raised a special-needs child
- ☐ Ran a 5K, 10K, or marathon
- ☐ Reached a weight goal
- ☐ Received an art or music award
- ☐ Restored a relationship
- ☐ Stopped smoking
- ☐ Other: _____
- ☐ Other: _____

Conversation Starters about Successes:

- What items did you check or write?
- Were you affirmed or applauded for one of your successes, even if it was with simple words of congratulations? Discuss.

OPTIONAL CONVERSATION ENHANCER

GOD'S DEFINITION OF SUCCESS

*For in Christ the fullness of God lives in a human body,
and you are complete through your union with Christ.
He is the Lord over every ruler and authority in the universe.*
(COLOSSIANS 2:9–10, NLT)

Born cross-eyed and legally blind in her left eye, Carole Brewer was ridiculed in school for her outward appearance. Her eye was straightened by surgery at age nine, but her low self-esteem didn't change until her senior year in college when she surrendered her heart to Jesus. Today, she is a recording artist, songwriter, worship leader, and speaker.

Carole says that her visual impairment reminds her of the problems she had in seeing the Lord. Now convicted by God's Word and led by his Holy Spirit, Carole's past spiritual blind spots and out-of-focus thinking have changed into a true perception of Jesus that is daily getting closer to the 20/20 vision she knows she will have in heaven.

God gifted Carole with a remarkable voice, a desire to follow him, and the ability to lead others into his presence. But, even as a Christian, Carole used to dread seeing herself on television because of the possibility that her fatigued left eye would turn in. One discouraging day, the Lord whispered to her, "It's okay Carole. Don't you know that there are others out there saying, 'Look, her eye does it too!'"

Overwhelmed by God's enormous love for her, Carole began to find her esteem in Christ, not in her lacking self. She says, "I'm glad that I never made any deals with Jesus like, 'Lord, if you heal my eye, I'll do this or that for you the rest of my life.' He has already paid the ultimate price for me, and I am now free to serve him generously from my grateful heart—whatever the circumstance—because of who he is and whose I am, not because of who I am or what marvelous things he has done for me."

Worth Chatting About: How do you feel about defining success as "union with Christ"?

So . . . What Are Your Final Thoughts about Successes?

- Talk to your Purpose Partner about what is clear to you today and what you still need clarified about the topic of success. What wisdom do you think God has shared with you?

TODAY'S THIRD TOPIC: MIRACLES

The greatest recurring miracle of my life is that God continues to use me in spite of my sinfulness. I stand utterly amazed that he would use someone like me to accomplish his purposes. What about you? Take some time to quiet your mind while you ask God to help you recall some of the hundreds of miracles that he has performed in your life or in the lives of your loved ones. The more specific you can be, by listing events or circumstances, the better—but frankly, there would be nothing wrong with praising God today for the miracle of sunsets! Write five of your favorite miracles.

REMEMBER THE MIRACLES

1. _____

2. _____

3. _____

4. _____

5. _____

Conversation Starters about Miracles:

- What miracles did you write? Describe your favorite one in more detail.
- Is there a limit to God's potential miracles in your life?

- What next miracle would you like to see God perform?

- Discuss together how it made you feel to remember some of the miracles God has done in your life and in the lives of your loved ones.

TODAY'S FOURTH TOPIC: PASSIONS

Discovering a healthy passion gives you a new lease on life. It creates an intensity in your personality at which people marvel. It may be a fun passion—international travel, off-roading, master gardening, rollerblading, or weight lifting. It may be that you are passionate about a specific cause, such as muscular dystrophy, illiteracy, restoration of historical landmarks, animal rights, or the passage of a school bond. If it's a spiritual passion, some might call it a magnificent obsession for the Lord. Perhaps that's pro-life education, helping couples rekindle their love, or evangelism. All healthy passions will bring you one step closer to finding your purpose in life, because all are a gift from God and have the potential of being used by him to spread the good news. Did you realize that?

Do you have a lighthearted passion or a heavy-duty one? It's reader's choice today! Either type of answer is great. Other than knowing Christ and growing your faith (which are "givens" as basic passions!), what can you spend hours on—without even realizing it?

Consider all these ways to ask yourself the same question about your healthy passions:

- What do I love to do?
- What makes me soar on wings like eagles?
- What do I get lost in for hours?
- What gives zest to my life?
- What do I love talking about?
- What is more valuable to me than gold?
- What would I rather be doing than anything else?
- What feels like play to me?
- What's my favorite hobby?

Check any items that apply to you or write your answer. In the "Unhealthy Passions" portion of the exercise, it's all right simply to make a mental note of any answers you feel uncomfortable recording in the workbook.

HEALTHY AND UNHEALTHY PASSIONS

Healthy Passions:

- [ ] Airplanes
- [ ] Anti-abortion education
- [ ] Archaeology
- [ ] Art
- [ ] Boating
- [ ] Bowling
- [ ] Cake decorating
- [ ] Children's books
- [ ] Classical music
- [ ] Cooking
- [ ] Crocheting
- [ ] Current events
- [ ] Deep-sea fishing
- [ ] Discipleship/evangelism
- [ ] Endangered species
- [ ] Folk dancing
- [ ] Forensic science
- [ ] Graphic design
- [ ] Grief therapy
- [ ] Health
- [ ] Hockey
- [ ] Horses
- [ ] Image makeovers
- [ ] Justice
- [ ] Kickboxing
- [ ] Loving abused children
- [ ] Mission trips

- [ ] Motorcycling
- [ ] Ozone layer damage
- [ ] Painting
- [ ] Piano
- [ ] Politics
- [ ] Puzzles
- [ ] Recovery program
- [ ] Remodeling
- [ ] Reptiles
- [ ] Rock climbing
- [ ] Safe neighborhoods
- [ ] Scuba diving
- [ ] Sewing
- [ ] Singing
- [ ] Single mothers
- [ ] Snowboarding
- [ ] Soup kitchens
- [ ] The unemployed
- [ ] TV decency ratings
- [ ] Volunteerism
- [ ] Women's rights
- [ ] Writing
- [ ] Youth ministry

- [ ] Other: _____
- [ ] Other: _____

Unhealthy Passions:

- Adultery
- Alcohol abuse
- Compulsive eating
- Constant shopping
- Constant talking on the telephone
- Control
- Gambling
- Nonprescription drugs
- Obsessive house cleaning
- Overspending
- Pornography
- Recklessness
- Self
- Television on day and night
- Other: _____
- Other: _____

Conversation Starter about Passions:

- What answer(s) did you check or write? Take some time to share some of your thoughts.

OPTIONAL CONVERSATION ENHANCER

PASSIONATE WITNESS FOR GOD

You have put gladness in my heart, more than when . . .
grain and new wine abound.
(PSALM 4:7, NASB)

Raised on the edge of poverty by a single mother, Allison Gappe Bottke started her life in the projects of Cleveland, Ohio. Early childhood molestation left her scarred. At the age of fifteen, she ran away from home and married a young man whose physical abuse nearly killed her. By sixteen, Allison was a divorced, single mother making her way through school on welfare. Much later, she became one of America's first full-figure models. It is through her personal U-turn story of spiritual redemption that she founded the "God Allows U-Turns" ministry. Allison believes that the Lord saved her from a turbulent life, so she could stand as a firm witness to the fact that no sin is too great that you can't turn around.

Allison has a passion to reach those who, like herself in years gone by, are stuck in turmoil and addiction. She says, "My past isn't pretty: teenage pregnancy, drugs, alcohol, abortion, and other poor choices. Today, I am passionate about how God can change a life when someone opens her heart to him. I love sharing how you can never be too lost or too broken to turn your heart toward God." Allison has a particularly soft spot for non-Christians and radical feminists entrenched in the New Age movement. She says, "Ask God to reveal himself to you today in a mighty way and to uncover a burning passion that he can use. Then go for it the rest of your life!"

Worth Chatting About: Why do you think God would entrust a passion to someone who previously made wrong choices?

Searching Scripture Together for Wisdom about Passions: Read Isaiah 1:1–20, which is the beginning of Isaiah's vision concerning Judah and Jerusalem. Isaiah was passionate about reaching the nation of Judah for God. He was God's messenger that the people should stop bringing meaningless offerings. **Something to Talk About:** Reflect on your passion—healthy or unhealthy—and talk about how God could possibly use it to reach people for him.

So . . . What Are Your Final Thoughts about Passions?

• What have you noticed about your passion or lack of it?

• Ask your Purpose Partner to comment about *her* greatest passion or lack of one.

Wrapping Up

PRAYER LOG:

Update your Prayer Log on page 140 as you share prayer requests and praise reports.

CLOSE YOUR TIME TOGETHER IN CONVERSATION WITH GOD:

Dear God, help us learn to enjoy more fully the fun side of our life purpose more. Thank you for finding creative ways to inspire us. Thank you for all the successes we have had, especially in knowing that our biggest victory is that we are complete through our union with Christ. Thank you for your generosity in performing modern-day miracles in our lives. And thank you that you have put gladness in our hearts with the healthy passions you instilled in us. We are more blessed than when grain, new wine, and your other provisions abound. We pray that we would live a passionate life for you today! We are tired of just existing day-to-day. Ignite a fire in us that uses our passions for the good of those you love. Help us spend more time with you, the Author of our inspiration, successes, miracles, and wholesome passions. In Jesus' name, we pray. Amen.

BEFORE YOUR NEXT CONVERSATION:

- Read the chapter and complete the exercises for Conversation #5.
- Pray diligently for your Purpose Partner's prayer requests, as well as your own. Spend time throughout the week praising God for who he is and for all he has done for both of you. Ask him for an extra measure of wisdom and discernment for your next conversation that addresses some good predictors of your future purposes.

Discussing Good Predictors of Your Future Purposes

Open Your Time Together in Conversation with God: *Dear God, today we ask for your extra measure of boldness as we discuss our ministry and mission work, life message, heart's burning desire, and sneak preview. We know that you care more about these things than even we do, so help us finish the race you set out before us by giving us more clarity on your pathway to purpose. In Jesus' name, we pray. Amen.*

Just for Fun: Share about the most interesting type of personality you've ever encountered. You might think of someone in one of these categories: a risk-taker, an introvert, a mad scientist, an eccentric, or a loud laugher. Have fun, but use a pseudonym to protect the privacy of the interesting type!

Today's First Topic: Ministry and Mission Work

There is no earthly explanation for why one ministry makes your heart sing and another does not. All we know for sure is that God made each individual unique, so that all the precious tasks he needed to accomplish in this world would get done by someone who loved doing them. For example, someone loves to paint and decorate Sunday school classrooms, while another thinks that building church websites is loads of fun.

Is your best time in ministry when you are giving your testimony at a new believers' coffee, providing child care for church members, coaching women, or writing plays for the youth ministry? Is it when you are directing traffic for weekend services, driving senior saints to their doctors' appointments, or serving as a hospital chaplain?

And, what about your heart for missions? Is your "thing" to deliver mosquito nets to Third World countries? Is it doing research for an international mission trip or anonymously donating funds for those who can't afford to go overseas without raising support? Is it planting churches in remote locations?

It's so important to be aware of the areas of service that do not drain you, because there will be plenty of all-hands-on-deck assignments that will wear you out when you are asked by God to handle them. Today, think about what service opportunities you have had in church ministry or mission work. Check any that apply to you or write your answer. Put an asterisk by your favorites.

MINISTRY AND MISSION OPPORTUNITIES

☐ Car repair ministry
☐ Church office volunteering
☐ College campus evangelism
☐ Mission trip abroad doing _____
☐ Mission work locally doing _____
☐ October harvest party
☐ Orphanage ministry
☐ Sewing ministry
☐ Small group leadership
☐ Worship band

☐ Other: _____

☐ Other: _____

Conversation Starters about Ministry and Missions:

- What answers did you give? Tell about several memorable times you have had while serving others. If you'd like, you also can tell about your least favorite experience.

- What do you think God has been teaching you through your ministry and mission opportunities or lack of them? Talk about whether you need to pray for God's advice about a specific next step. If you do, stop and pray a simple prayer now.

OPTIONAL CONVERSATION ENHANCER

FINDING YOUR SERVICE NICHE

The King will reply, "I tell you the truth, whatever you did for one of the least of these brothers of mine, you did for me."
(MATTHEW 25:40)

Pat Palau is a cross-cultural evangelist with her husband, Luis, and the Luis Palau Evangelistic Association. She is a wife and mother of four married sons and nine grandchildren, who contributes to a peaceful home base for her family.

Pat has been humbled by a growing sphere of ministry influence in recent years, both on her own and in conjunction with the festivals and crusades the Association sponsors. She says that her husband shows people how to become Christians and she believes that she makes their growing in the faith less complicated. Having been on a long, wonderful ride with Jesus, she finds enormous joy in sharing biblical insights on God's will and his ways.

Pat has noticed over the years that, even though she has spoken in many venues in many countries, she loves, above all else, to speak at women's weekend retreats. She says that the personal interaction, the flow of teaching, and the freedom to say all she knows about God's grace gives her a deep sense of satisfaction. She says, "There is nothing better than letting our love of Jesus spill into our faith in words and action. It is exhilarating to say and do things that help people grow into God's plan for their lives."

Worth Chatting About: What service opportunity do you wish you had had or still want to have?

TODAY'S SECOND TOPIC: LIFE MESSAGE

It's uncanny how God has given each one of us a life message to share with our hurting world. That message entrusted to us makes us God's messengers. The delivery of his message makes us his faithful ambassadors. For the exercise on page 81, "Special Edition: The Times," fill in today's date and your name. Then, write what you would tell the world, if you knew that everyone would immediately do whatever you told them to do. (Yes . . . when [your name here] speaks, everyone listens!)

Don't write a generic salvation message. Make it more specific to your personalized vision from God or the dream of your heart. For example,

- Be kind to the unlovely.
- Don't ever give up.
- Forgive others.
- Love unconditionally with Jesus' love.
- Never lose your hope in God.
- Be joyful always.

THE TIMES

DATE: _____

"What I'd Like to Tell the World."

According to _____, **Leading Life Plan Strategist:**

"

"

Conversation Starters about Your Life Message:

- What did you write and why?

- Talk to each other about how this exercise made you feel (for example: overwhelmed, afraid, confused, hopeful, excited). Why do you think that happened?

Today's Third Topic: Heart's Burning Desire

Have you been told that you should leave a legacy, follow your destiny, or make a difference with your life? Have you ever been asked, "What is your contribution going to be?" These phrases capture an important insight about human nature: We want our lives to matter; we want to leave an impact on our world. Of course, God created you with that human nature, and he *does* have something for you to do while you're here on earth.

What if there were no guidelines as to what you could do with and for God? What if you had unlimited resources, including all the time, money, and energy you needed? Let today's exercise liberate you. Allow it to help you think outside all your normal boundaries about what God might have in mind for your life. For now, the sky's the limit!

Would you fund shelters for abused children, develop a national prayer ministry to support fire and medical personnel, or generously adopt several elderly couples as your grandparents? What if God was 100 percent supportive of your idea? Would you write wholesome children's books, establish accredited training centers to raise up more Christian school teachers, open a food bank in a low-income neighborhood, or sponsor dream vacations for pastors and their families? Would you pour every resource you had into finding a cure for a disease, teaching people to glorify God, or nestling the orphans of the world into families? Would you start a drug recovery ministry in your church, open a women's life purpose center, or lobby against internet pornography?

You might think about your heart's burning desire in any of the following ways:

- What is my deepest longing? (You may never have told another living soul!)
- What do I yearn for, hunger for, or crave? (No, not food!)
- What do I hope for or wish?
- What do I want to contribute?

- What do I want to be recognized for? (Not the best motive in the world, but it may trigger a useful thought!)
- What cause or people-group breaks my heart?
- What would I do or be if I had all the money and influence in the world?

Check your heart's desire or write your answer.

MY HEART'S BURNING DESIRE

☐ Be financially secure
☐ Cure a disease
☐ Get married
☐ Have a child
☐ Publish a book
☐ Travel

☐ Other: _____

☐ Other: _____

Conversation Starters about Your Heart's Burning Desire:

- What is your heart's burning desire? What details do you know about it?
- How long have you felt this way?

OPTIONAL CONVERSATION ENHANCER
OUTRAGEOUS, NO-LIMITS DREAMS!

His master replied, "Well done, good and faithful servant! . . . Come and share your master's happiness!"
(MATTHEW 25:21)

Renée Bondi is a wife, mother, classroom helper, daughter, sister, daughter-in-law, godmother, neighbor, and in-demand speaker, author, and recording artist. Renée's relationship with Jesus has grown deeper as she continues to recognize him in the little things as well as the traumatic.

In 1988, two months shy of her wedding day, Renée was in a freak accident that left her a quadriplegic. One year after her five-month hospital stay, during which Renée underwent surgery to fuse her neck bones and received occupational therapy, she married her longtime sweetheart, Mike.

What is Renée's dream? She would love to reclaim our culture for Christ by going into high schools, colleges, and churches using all possible resources to nurture great screenwriters, film producers, recording artists, journalists, and visual artists who would infiltrate our society with clean, positive entertainment. She would then build a tremendous marketing machine that would heavily promote such "roaring lambs." She says, "Blow the lid off the box in which you have stuffed God. I am astounded by what he has done with this broken body so far—with emphasis on the words *so far!*"

Worth Chatting About: Why is it a good idea to blow the lid off the box in which you have stuffed God?

Searching Scripture Together for Wisdom about Following Your Heart's Desire: Read Luke 8:1–3 about women like Mary Magdalene, Joanna the wife of Cuza (who was the manager of Herod's household), Susanna, and many others who loved Jesus and found deep joy in financially supporting his ministry.

Something to Talk About: When you get to heaven, will God count you among those who, in support of his ministry, followed your heart's desire?

So . . . What Are Your Final Thoughts about Your Heart's Burning Desire?

- Talk about how it felt to write down your heart's burning desire. Discuss the fact that God puts his best desires in human beings.

TODAY'S FOURTH TOPIC: SNEAK PREVIEW

God often gives immediate marching orders for kingdom-building tasks he assigns, but sometimes he reveals a sneak preview of a far-off season in a person's life. If he chose to give you an early peek at one of your future assignments, he might have wanted to give you time to muster courage, stamina, character, and resources—so that when the time came for your ministry to unfold, you wouldn't be terrified or ill-prepared. An early glimpse of your life's calling can help you long for it and more graciously accept it. Habakkuk 2:3 (NLT) says, "But these things I plan won't happen right away. Slowly, steadily, surely, the time approaches when the vision will be fulfilled." You must be careful, though, not to grow impatient once you've seen a preview. As you probe this idea today, have fun answering the questions on pages 86–87.

GOD'S SNEAK PREVIEW FOR ME?

1. What did you dream of being or doing when you were growing up? _____
   _____

   What attracted you to that career, role, ministry, mission, or avocation?

   _____

   _____

   _____

   Has that dream come true, at least in part? _____

   Explain. _____

   _____

   _____

   Is it likely that it will ever come true? _____

   Explain. _____

   _____

2. What were your favorite and least favorite subjects in school?

   Favorite: _____ _____

   Least Favorite: _____ _____

3. What were some of your favorite childhood pastimes? _____

   _____ _____

4. What were you good at as a child? _____

   Later in life? _____

5. What has been one of your favorite life experiences? _____

Regarding that experience, what did you notice was your most obvious weakness?_____

_____

Explain. _____

6. Over the years, what have you been affirmed for? _____
Explain. _____

7. If you had inherited one billion, tax-free dollars five years ago, how do you think you would have furthered God's kingdom on earth? _____

_____

8. Over the years, what has God been nudging you to do about joyfully fulfilling his purposes for your life? _____

_____

9. Have you seen a glimpse of your next, immediate purpose?_____
If so, what did you see? _____

_____

Conversation Starters about Sneak Previews:

- How did you answer the nine questions?

- Not everything from childhood, or even adulthood, is a sneak preview, nor do we want to force any conclusions. Some things are just circumstances of life. That said, which of your answers might have an element of a sneak preview?

- Do you think it would be harder to have or not to have a sneak preview of one of your biggest assignments?

Wrapping Up

Prayer Log:

Update your Prayer Log on page 140 as you share prayer requests and praise reports.

Close Your Time Together in Conversation with God:

Dear God, we pray that we will live the rest of our days humbly and joyfully serving those you love both in our church and beyond its doors. And we ask for an extra measure of your grace, because we want to serve you well on our mission field, until our dying breath. Nothing would give us a greater privilege than delivering the message you sent us into the world to deliver. We also pray that you will extend favor to us in regard to what you are laying on our hearts to do with you and for you. Today we pray that you will grant the unfolding of our God-centered visions, with or without any sneak previews! In Jesus' name, we pray. Amen.

Before Your Next Conversation:

- Think about how you and your Purpose Partner could enjoy a few hours off together during Conversation #7, *Taking a Laughter Break*. The choice for an adventure is yours. (See page 49 for suggestions.) Whatever suits your fancy, whether that's searching for your favorite perfume fragrance or smelling roses in a garden, plan on finalizing the details of your outing during Conversation #6.
- Read the chapter and complete the exercises for Conversation #6.
- Pray diligently for your Purpose Partner's prayer requests, as well as your own. Spend time throughout the week praising God for who he is and for all he has done for both of you. Don't be shy about asking him to help you with your "Tough Questions" homework and to be present at your next conversation.

ANSWERING SOME TOUGH QUESTIONS

Open Your Time Together in Conversation with God: *Dear God, today we ask for your truth as we try to answer some tough questions. We know that you are the only one who can shine light on our human answers and inspire us toward your point of view. In Jesus' name, we pray. Amen.*

Just for Fun: Share about your favorite book, concert, play, movie, or television program.

OPTIONAL CONVERSATION ENHANCER

WHAT NEGATIVE LIFE PATTERN WOULD YOU LIKE TO INTERRUPT?

Search me, O God, and know my heart; test me and know my anxious thoughts. See if there is any offensive way in me, and lead me in the way everlasting.
(PSALM 139:23-24)

Peggy Campolo has been married to Tony for nearly a half of a century. She has edited thirty of his books and has always enthusiastically supported his ministry and missionary calling. Her professional experience includes teaching first grade, working in public relations, and selling real estate. She was a full-time mother to their son and daughter, and now enjoys four grand-children, in addition to writing and speaking about the grace and love of Jesus Christ. Her favorite audiences and protégés are those who have not felt loved, have not been accepted by God's other children, or have not been wel-comed in the church.

Peggy says that one of her longtime, negative life patterns was that she tended to react on the basis of what other people told her or to fall back on what she had always thought. Later, she learned to more often let the Holy Spirit guide her thinking and actions. She now says, "Once you get stuck in a negative pattern, it takes a mighty leap of faith to take the hand of the Holy Spirit and do your best to follow God's leading out of the pattern that feels like it is set in stone. Don't just drift into life patterns; choose them wisely."

Worth Chatting About: What negative life pattern would *you* like to interrupt?

TODAY'S ONLY EXERCISE: 30 TOUGH QUESTIONS

Write your answers without overanalyzing them.

1. How do you react to criticism? Why do you think you react that way? _____

_____

2. Who are you?

I am _____

I am not _____

3. Are you getting lazy or too comfortable? Why do you say that? _____

_____

4. Do you usually ask for what you want? Why or why not? _____

_____

5. Do you have a personal sense of peace? If so, how do you nurture that peacefulness? If not, why do you think you don't have peace? _____

_____

6. What do you need to hear in your life, more than anything else? Do you typically hear it? _____

_____

7. Has your life become too busy? If yes, what steps can you take to change that? If no, how do you maintain the balance? _____

_____

8. What are you bracing yourself for? What is the likelihood it will happen? _____

_____

9. If you did what was really on your heart to do, who would try to dissuade you and why? _____

_____

10. Who was or is an antagonist, villain, enemy, or bad guy in your life? Have you allowed that person to control your kingdom contributions? _____

_____

11. Where's your leverage? In other words, what do you know, have, own, or represent that gives you an advantage that many others don't have? _____

_____

12. What sin do you need to confess? (It's okay to write it in secret code. God can decode!) _____

13. Do you feel as if you are following your destiny or wandering through life? Why? _____

_____

14. What have you contributed to your church and community?

Church: _____

Community: _____

15. What would you like written on your tombstone? (Some possibilities follow.) Write your epitaph on the line below:

A difference maker   One who cared

Devoted spouse   She passed on what she could figure out

Faithful friend   Trusted advisor

God used her up   Woman who risked everything

Loyal to the end   Woman with fire in her belly

Your Epitaph: _____

16. How can you make a difference in the world you know today? _____

_____

17. If there were no God, heaven, or hell, what would you do with the rest of your life? _____

_____

_____

18. What difficult task do you need to do? Are you willing to do it, even if you are afraid? If not, why not? _____

_____

19. Is there something you are doing that you need to walk away from? If yes, what is it? _____

20. If you could have one wish come true, what would it be? _____

_____

21. Is your heart in your current projects, or are you uninspired right now? Explain.

_____

22. What ideas are you in love with that might prevent you from seeing truth clearly? _____

_____

23. What was the hardest decision you ever had to make? _____

_____

24. What is your gut directing you to do that you have been ignoring? _____

_____

25. What is your purpose-in-life (your primary life role, whether that is in your family, career, or ministry) during this season of your life? _____

_____

26. What are you trying to find? Do you expect to find it? _____

_____

27. As you look at your life story, at what point would you say a new chapter began for you? _____

28. If you could fix one thing currently broken in your life, what would that be and what would you do about it? _____

_____

29. What is calling your name? _____

_____

30. Where have you been? Where would you like to go? (There are many interpretations of this question—you choose.) _____

_____

Conversation Starters about Your 30 Tough Questions:

- Discuss together your answers to the 30 Tough Questions.

- What answer(s) surprised you, concerned you, confused you?

- If you had a chance to do something in your life over again, what would it be?

- What new insights or questions has this exercise raised?

- Discuss the final details of your Laughter Break: date, time, place, who's driving, and so on.

Wrapping Up

Prayer Log:

Update your Prayer Log on page 141 as you share prayer requests and praise reports.

Close Your Time Together in Conversation with God:

Dear God, thank you for being a true and encouraging friend during this chat today. Answering these questions was not easy, but we are both anxious to see more truth in our lives. We don't want to "do life" without you. In Jesus' name, we pray. Amen.

Before Your Next Conversation:

- Call your Purpose Partner to reconfirm all the details of your play day. Make sure you have each other's home and cell phone numbers with you in case a last-minute emergency prevents you from meeting.
- Because Conversation #7 is a play day, don't forget later to prepare for Conversation #8, by reading the chapter and completing the exercises.
- Pray diligently for your Purpose Partner's prayer requests, as well as your own. Spend time throughout the week praising God for who he is and for all he has done for both of you. Invite him to join you on your Laughter Break, as you and your Purpose Partner have fun goofing off together!

Taking a Laughter Break

Before you gear up for your last three important appointments, you have an official day off from processing information to go and have fun with your Purpose Partner. There should be no talking about life purpose during this outing—only laughing and enjoying each other's company! Don't forget to pray as you start and end your adventure.

Some Questions to Ponder This Week:

- How often do you usually have fun or play?
- What does that response tell you about yourself?
- What does the inclusion of a laughter break in this life-purpose book tell you about the importance of relaxing (hints: pacing yourself; enjoying the journey)?

Before Your Next Conversation:

- Read the chapter and complete the exercises for Conversation #8. Because it is more involved than previous preparation and much more critical to seeing the big picture, please allow adequate time—at least an hour.

- Pray diligently for your Purpose Partner's previous or current prayer requests, as well as your own. Spend time throughout the week praising God for who he is and for all he has done for both of you. Ask him simply to change your perspective into his perspective. Tell him that you are ready to cooperate with any changes that are necessary for fulfilling your life purposes. Then, look forward to what he will do before, during, and after your next conversation.

Part Three

Seeing *the* *Bigger* Picture

*Don't become so well-adjusted to your culture that you fit
into it without even thinking. Instead, fix your attention on God.
You'll be changed from the inside out. Readily recognize what
he wants from you, and quickly respond to it. Unlike the culture
around you, always dragging you
down to its level of immaturity,
God brings the best out of you,
develops well-formed maturity
in you.*

(Romans 12:2, MSG)

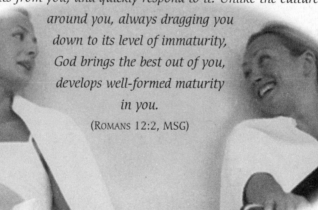

MAKING PERSPECTIVE
WORK FOR YOU

Open Your Time Together in Conversation with God: *Dear God, today we ask for your broad perspective. We tend to see things the same way we've always seen them. We now want to see our life as you see it, as you would like it to be. Enlarge our view as we analyze our perspective and attempt to change it, as needed. In Jesus' name, we pray. Amen.*

Just for Fun: Share something about your first job, first day of school, or first date.

Quick Review: You pondered several questions last week; discuss them today with your Purpose Partner . . .

• How often do you usually have fun or play?

• What does that response tell you about yourself?

• What does the inclusion of a laughter break in this life-purpose book tell you about the importance of relaxing?

TODAY'S FIRST EXERCISE

Transfer some of your favorite, previous answers from Conversations #1–5 to the summary chart on pages 102–104. It will give you an at-a-glance look at your life when you analyze your perspective with your Purpose Partner.

For example:

Grief	Divorce	Mom's death
	Job layoff	Lupus
Successes	CPR certification	High school class officer
	Backpacked Europe	Article published

PERSPECTIVE SUMMARY CHART: WHO AM I?

Relationships
(page 29)

_____   _____

_____   _____

Characteristics
(pages 31–33)

_____   _____

_____   _____

Roles
(page 38)

_____   _____

_____   _____

Core Values and Beliefs
(pages 41–42)

_____   _____

_____   _____

Spiritual Habits
(page 44)

_____   _____

_____   _____

Strengths
(pages 46–47)

_____   _____

_____   _____

Motives
(pages 52–53)

_____   _____

_____   _____

Fear
(pages 55–56)

_____   _____

_____   _____

Grief
(page 58)

_____   _____

_____   _____

Mistaken Thinking
(page 61)

_____   _____

_____   _____

Inspiration
(pages 66–67)

_____   _____

_____   _____

Successes
(page 68)

_____   _____

_____   _____

Miracles
(page 70)

_____   _____

_____   _____

Passions
(pages 72–73)

_____   _____

_____   _____

Ministry and Mission Work
(page 78)

_____   _____

_____   _____

Life Message
(page 81)

_____   _____

_____   _____

Heart's Burning Desire
(page 83)

_____   _____

_____   _____

Sneak Preview
(pages 86–87)

_____   _____

_____   _____

Conversation Starters about Who You Are:

- Share your answers, postponing your comments until the next exercise.

- Talk about what surprised you when you saw your life laid out in this format. (Again, reserve other comments.)

TODAY'S SECOND EXERCISE: ANALYZING YOUR PERSPECTIVE SUMMARY CHART

Take a couple of minutes to review your answers to the "30 Tough Questions" exercise in Conversation #6 (pages 90–94). With that information fresh in your mind, browse through your "Perspective Summary Chart." Don't focus on the spaces you left blank, or you'll have to write "highly self-critical" under Characteristics! Instead, enjoy all the ones you filled in.

You will notice that who you are inherently—at your core—has nothing to do with your outer trappings. For example, "gorgeous hair" didn't hold much weight on your perspective chart, did it? You are obviously not the sum total of your clothing, the square footage of your home, the make of your car, the limit on your credit cards, or the accomplishments of your children. Being rich or poor did not count for much in relation to other things on the perspective list, did it? This chart truly represents who you are.

You might have noticed in doing this exercise that your past is not changeable and that most of your roles and talents are fairly set for this season, but did you realize that some of the rest of who you are *is* changeable? As you complete the following analysis, try not to compare yourself to others—because you've just shown how unique you are! No one has the same life history or life design as you do. Remember that always.

PERSPECTIVE SUMMARY ANALYSIS

1. Star three things on your "Perspective Summary Chart" currently going well in your life—for example, something that you're proud of, that is encouraging to you, that's captured your heart, or that you see as a valuable asset. Something positive.

2. Circle one thing on your "Perspective Summary Chart" that you are *not* happy with, but that you are almost fully able to change. In other words, what negative part of your life would you like to work on: a relationship, motive, fear, grief issue, mistaken thinking, or other?

   Now, check or write a specific statement that describes the negativity with which you're unhappy.

   ☐ I am refusing to forgive someone or something.

   ☐ Mistaken thinking has been keeping me miserable because I didn't know old scripts could be erased.

   ☐ I'm not in sync, in step, with my current roles in life.

   ☐ I've grown used to abuse, depression, temper, or addiction. It takes too much energy to change.

   ☐ I have allowed my grief to make me bitter.

   ☐ I have forgotten how to dream passionately.

(continued)

☐ I'm compromising my values, and that's tearing at my heart.

☐ Other: _____

You now have two choices about what you circled and described: To say, "Maybe I'll get around to working on that someday." Or, you can commit to taking one baby step today toward a solution. If you have decided to take an action step now, write that step here! _____

_____

3. Reread your answers about your strengths, successes, passions, ministry and mission work, life message, heart's burning desire, and sneak preview. These are all trustworthy indicators as to what you'll contribute with your life. Now, ask yourself: "If I did not doubt and fear, how could I make a difference?"

_____

_____

4. Ask yourself: "Have I been ignoring the truth of what God wants of me?"
☐ Yes   ☐ No

If yes, what is it that you are supposed to be doing or being? _____

_____

If no, how have you been worrying too much? _____

_____

5. As you skim over your answers, can you tell if you have ever felt, in the past, that God was using you in his service?
☐ Yes   ☐ No

If yes, when and how? _____

If no, why do you think that is so? _____

6. Based on what you now know, do you want to be used by God now?

☐ Yes ☐ No

Why or why not? _____

7. How would you specifically like to serve—if the world were your oyster? _____

_____

8. What do you think your second-half-of-life assignment might be? _____

_____

Conversation Starters about Analyzing Your Perspective Summary Chart:

• What did you write? Talk about your answers.

• Discuss together any insights about this exercise. Where might you need God's direction? Challenge one another to understand that God, in his wisdom, knows exactly how to use all the information in your perspective chart to accomplish his work on earth.

Today's Third Exercise: Changing Your Perspective

Answer the questions by checking any items that apply or by writing your answer.

Changing My Perspective

1. Breaking out of the rut of your routine can greatly affect your perspective. What two, fun, specific things can you do to help change your perspective and interrupt negative patterns? (The more lighthearted the answer about how to get unstuck, the better. Do not list the more serious methods like prayer, Bible reading, and listening to God. We've already covered those in detail in *Pathway to Purpose for Women*, and they are assumed here.)

    ☐ Eat dessert first in a restaurant.

    ☐ Shop at a different grocery store.

    ☐ Shower in my pajamas (just because I can!).

    ☐ Sit at a different seat at the dinner table.

    ☐ Tour a garbage dump.

    ☐ Visit a spa with hot-water springs.

    ☐ Walk up the stairs backward.

    ☐ Wear my watch on the wrong wrist.

    ☐ Other: _____

2. Since Conversation #1 of this journey, what new perspectives have you been developing?

☐ Instant gratification is a serious disease today.

☐ I shouldn't minister if I don't support my ministry with prayer.

☐ It is time to serve out of love, not duty.

☐ My ministry matters to God.

☐ Relationships are one of God's greatest gifts to me.

☐ Other: _____

3. What new pattern will you now practice?

☐ Get some form of physical exercise.

☐ Get up earlier to spend some quiet time with God.

☐ Proactively avoid gossip.

☐ Question my values and beliefs every so often.

☐ Stop abusing drugs, alcohol, nicotine, or food.

☐ Stop cursing.

☐ Stop obsessing.

☐ Other: _____

Conversation Starters about Changing Your Perspective:

• What did you check or write? Talk about your answers.

• Discuss together what you think God has been trying to say to you through this exercise.

Wrapping Up

PRAYER LOG:

Update your Prayer Log on page 141 as you share prayer requests and praise reports.

CLOSE YOUR TIME TOGETHER IN CONVERSATION WITH GOD:

Dear God, thank you for being a huge part of our analysis today. Your clear perspective means more to us than anything else! Change our perspective as you see fit. Things are beginning to make sense according to your plan. Keep us on the right track, so we will follow your will for our lives. In Jesus' name, we pray. Amen.

BEFORE YOUR NEXT CONVERSATION

- Read the chapter and complete the exercises for Conversation #9.
- Pray diligently for your Purpose Partner's prayer requests, as well as your own. Spend time throughout the week praising God for who he is and for all he has done for both of you. Pray intently for your willingness to surrender whatever he asks of you in your next preparation time or conversation.

SURRENDERING

Open Your Time Together in Conversation with God: *Dear God, today we ask for your direction in the area of our surrender to you. We know that this will not be an easy topic, so we want to pray for your peace that surpasses understanding as we make some hard decisions about submitting to your will, your ways, and your purposes for our lives. In Jesus' name, we pray. Amen.*

Just for fun: Share with each other about an adventure you had on a vacation or outing.

TODAY'S ONLY TOPIC: SURRENDER

Surrender is the willingness to give something to God and entrust it to his care. It means that you are ready to wave the white flag, releasing control as ruler of your universe and believing that God will do a better job. It is an acknowledgment that you are simply the steward of all he has asked you to manage for him on earth. Surrendering your life to God is the key to living out his purposes and fulfilling his plan for you.

Today's exercise is really only between God and you. Your Purpose Partner's role will be to encourage you, not to judge you. Check any areas of your life that you have already surrendered to God or are ready to surrender now, or write your answer. Please pray before making any decisions because

God may indeed take what you surrender to him. This prayerful thought process is called counting the cost and is not meant to make you afraid, only to make you aware.

SURRENDER INVENTORY

Personal Life

Financial:
- ☐ Budget
- ☐ Car(s)
- ☐ Credit cards
- ☐ Debt
- ☐ Education fund
- ☐ Financial margin
- ☐ Home (house, apartment)
- ☐ Income
- ☐ Needs
- ☐ Possessions
- ☐ Retirement account
- ☐ Savings
- ☐ Spending habits
- ☐ Travel opportunities
- ☐ Wants
- ☐ Other: _____
- ☐ Other: _____

Social/Relational:
- ☐ Accountability partners
- ☐ Argumentative spirit
- ☐ Best friend
- ☐ Fame
- ☐ Healthy/treasured relationships
- ☐ Heart
- ☐ Heroes
- ☐ Hobbies
- ☐ Inability to laugh, play, or relax
- ☐ Lack of authenticity
- ☐ Mentors
- ☐ Neighbors
- ☐ Passive aggression
- ☐ Popularity
- ☐ Protégés
- ☐ Reputation
- ☐ Support system
- ☐ Teachers
- ☐ Unhealthy relationships
- ☐ Vulnerability
- ☐ Other: _____
- ☐ Other: _____

Mental:
- ☐ Abilities
- ☐ Conflicts
- ☐ Control/manipulation
- ☐ Creativity
- ☐ Degrees/education
- ☐ Failures
- ☐ Favorite methods of self-sabotage
- ☐ Hopes, dreams, longings
- ☐ Ideas
- ☐ Impure motives
- ☐ Inappropriate books, magazines, movies

- [ ] Injustices
- [ ] Mind/will
- [ ] Most prized excuses
- [ ] Negative childhood scripts
- [ ] Perfectionism
- [ ] Personal power
- [ ] Perspective
- [ ] Positive and negative life experiences
- [ ] Self-righteousness
- [ ] Successes/ accomplishments
- [ ] Talents
- [ ] Temperament/disposition
- [ ] Victim mentality
- [ ] Other: _____
- [ ] Other: _____

Physical:
- [ ] Abuse (physical or sexual)
- [ ] Body
- [ ] Disability
- [ ] Eating disorder
- [ ] Energy level
- [ ] Exercise
- [ ] Healing
- [ ] Health
- [ ] Hormones
- [ ] Image
- [ ] Injury or accident
- [ ] Medication(s)
- [ ] Obesity
- [ ] Pain/suffering
- [ ] Safety
- [ ] Skills
- [ ] Slovenliness
- [ ] Sports
- [ ] Vanity
- [ ] Other: _____
- [ ] Other: _____

Emotional:
- [ ] All feelings
- [ ] Anxiety
- [ ] Depression
- [ ] Despair/grief/ sorrow
- [ ] Disappointment
- [ ] Fear(s)
- [ ] Frustration
- [ ] Guilt
- [ ] Happiness
- [ ] Hatred
- [ ] Hypersensitivity
- [ ] Inhibition(s)
- [ ] Jealousy
- [ ] Joy
- [ ] Memories (happy/sad)
- [ ] Passion (healthy/ unhealthy)
- [ ] Prejudice
- [ ] Regret
- [ ] Self-esteem
- [ ] Self-hate
- [ ] Shame
- [ ] Unbridled anger
- [ ] Worry
- [ ] Other: _____
- [ ] Other: _____

Family

- [ ] Abortion
- [ ] Blended family dynamics
- [ ] Crisis/tragedy/ illness/death
- [ ] Divorce
- [ ] Empty nest
- [ ] Ex-husband
- [ ] Family's mental/ physical health
- [ ] Family's safety/ finances/ life choices

- [ ] Family's salvation/joy
- [ ] Forgiveness
- [ ] Grandchild(ren)
- [ ] Grown-up kid(s)
- [ ] Heritage
- [ ] Infertility
- [ ] In-laws
- [ ] Intimacy
- [ ] Marriage
- [ ] Miscarriage
- [ ] Motherhood
- [ ] Parent(s)

- [ ] Premarital sex/ adultery
- [ ] Relatives
- [ ] Reunions
- [ ] Separation
- [ ] Sibling(s)
- [ ] Spouse
- [ ] Teen(s)
- [ ] Traditions
- [ ] Young child(ren)

- [ ] Other: _____
- [ ] Other: _____

Spiritual Growth and Faith

Spiritual Disciplines and Practice:

- [ ] Baptism
- [ ] Bible study
- [ ] Confession
- [ ] Discipleship
- [ ] Fasting
- [ ] Forgiveness
- [ ] Obedience
- [ ] Personal testimony

- [ ] Private worship
- [ ] Purity
- [ ] Quiet time/praying
- [ ] Sabbath
- [ ] Scripture memorization
- [ ] Silence
- [ ] Small group

- [ ] Spiritual journaling
- [ ] Tithing
- [ ] Trust/believing
- [ ] Witnessing

- [ ] Other: _____
- [ ] Other: _____

Church Involvement:

- [ ] Fellowship
- [ ] Leadership role
- [ ] Ministry(ies)

- [ ] Persecution for beliefs
- [ ] Public worship
- [ ] Servant's heart
- [ ] Spiritual gifts

- [ ] Other: _____
- [ ] Other: _____

Sins/Character Faults:

- [ ] Bitterness
- [ ] Foul mouth (cursing)
- [ ] Impatience
- [ ] Laziness
- [ ] Legalism
- [ ] Lust
- [ ] Lying
- [ ] Pride
- [ ] Rage
- [ ] Selfishness
- [ ] Sexual perversion
- [ ] Temper
- [ ] Other: _____
- [ ] Other: _____

Addictions, Compulsions, and Obsessions:

- [ ] Alcohol
- [ ] Cleaning
- [ ] Drugs
- [ ] Food
- [ ] Gossip
- [ ] Nicotine
- [ ] Pornography
- [ ] Sex
- [ ] Shopping
- [ ] Television
- [ ] Other: _____
- [ ] Other: _____

Vocation/Avocation

Career or Job:

- [ ] Awards
- [ ] Benefits package
- [ ] Boss
- [ ] Concepts
- [ ] Deadlines
- [ ] Employees
- [ ] Managerial roles
- [ ] Network
- [ ] Office politics
- [ ] Professional organizations
- [ ] Salary/raises
- [ ] Specific projects
- [ ] Strategic conversations
- [ ] Teamwork
- [ ] Other: _____
- [ ] Other: _____

Entrepreneurial Business Details:

- [ ] Capital expenditures
- [ ] Contracts
- [ ] Difficult employee(s)
- [ ] Loan(s)
- [ ] Marketing campaign
- [ ] Payroll
- [ ] Power lunches
- [ ] Profits
- [ ] Quarterly taxes
- [ ] Other: _____
- [ ] Other: _____

Mission Field

- [ ] Community contribution (schools, sports, charities, politics, arts)
- [ ] Missionary
- [ ] Personal comfort
- [ ] Self-sacrifice
- [ ] Willingness to serve locally or abroad
- [ ] Other: _____
- [ ] Other: _____

Life Purpose/Calling

- [ ] Current life roles
- [ ] Effort
- [ ] God's future plans
- [ ] Need for fulfillment/significance
- [ ] Perseverance
- [ ] Preconceived notions
- [ ] Other: _____
- [ ] Other: _____

Multiple Areas of Life

- [ ] All affirmations/recognition
- [ ] All allocations of time (busyness)
- [ ] All distractions
- [ ] All expectations
- [ ] All goals/visions/dreams
- [ ] All incredible opportunities
- [ ] All personal/group dynamics
- [ ] All resources
- [ ] All DECISIONS!
- [ ] Other: _____
- [ ] Other: _____

Take your everyday, ordinary life—
your sleeping, eating, going-to-work, and walking-around life—
and place it before God as an offering.

(ROMANS 12:1, MSG)

Pray the following prayer if you are ready to surrender one or more things on the list. Take this step at your own pace, without feeling rushed or pressured into it.

Today, I Surrender

Dear God,

I have counted the cost of surrendering the things I have indicated in the above inventory. I know full well that you may indeed take one or more of these things from me literally. I understand that, if you do, it is my responsibility to trust and obey you on a daily, hourly, and minute-by-minute basis. I know that you are acutely aware of how important these things are to me. I love you unconditionally as my Almighty Lord.

In your Son's holy name, I surrender these things. Amen.

_____   _____
Signature   Date

Continue Praying This Prayer If You Are Ready to Surrender Everything:

I am content with whatever you choose to give to me or take from me, whether you decide to bless me anymore or not. Everything I have belongs to you, so I leave it all in your hands. Give me the grace to never stop loving you, even if I . . .

- Lose everything, family included

- Am dirt poor

- Will never be considered a success

- Become terminally ill

- Will never see my dreams come true

- Will never feel like I am making a profound difference in the world

I freely empty myself of everything except you in order to be filled by you.

_____
(Your initials)

Conversation Starters about Surrender:

- What did you check or write? Because this is today's only exercise, feel free to talk leisurely about each of your answers, thought processes, and feelings.

- Discuss together one big thing you think God is trying to say to you through this exercise.

Wrapping Up

Prayer Log:

Update your Prayer Log on page 141 as you share prayer requests and praise reports.

Close Your Time Together in Conversation with God:

Dear God, thank you for what you revealed to us today about what you'd like us to surrender. You know that we began this exercise with many concerns, so thank you for your mercy and patience with our difficulties. In Jesus' name, we pray. Amen.

Before Your Next Conversation:

- Read the chapter and complete the exercises for Conversation #10.
- Pray diligently for your Purpose Partner's prayer requests, as well as your own. Spend time throughout the week praising God for who he is and for all he has done for both of you. Make this your most prayerful week of all, as your reflection time and next conversation point your farther down God's pathway to purpose.

FOLLOWING GOD'S PATHWAY TO PURPOSE

Open Your Last Time Together in Conversation with God:
Dear God, today we ask for more faith. Help us believe that you are who you say you are and that you do have a plan for our lives. We say that we believe, but when it comes to having faith that moves mountains, we find ourselves lacking. Lord, also help us to process our feelings about fulfilling our purposes through the various phases of your revelation to us. And, give us clear direction about which action steps to take in doing your will. In Jesus' name, we pray. Amen.

Just for Fun: Share about the funniest, happiest, or most unexpected thing that happened this month.

TODAY'S FIRST EXERCISE: BELIEVE!

Hebrews 11 features a list of our faithful ancestors in God's "hall of fame." It is a summary of those Old Testament men and women who boldly believed in God and his promises to them. Similarly, this exercise will help you determine whether you believe that God really does have a remarkable plan for your life. As you read this Bible passage with your Purpose Partner . . .

- Notice the perseverance of each person, in spite of the fears or dangers he or she faced.

- Notice the concept of a promised land, as well as God's delayed, greater promise for us to be made perfect at the resurrection.
- Notice God's commendations and rewards (such as an old couple having a baby, the Red Sea parting, and city walls falling down) for those who believed that he exists and who trusted him.
- Notice the extreme conditions, such as a nontransportable boat being built on dry land, a man giving up the wealth of Egypt, and people being tortured for what they believed—to the point of refusing to go free!

FOURTEEN PRINCIPLES OF LIVING BY FAITH
(Hebrews 11:1–40)

Answer the questions related to the fourteen concepts:

One: Have illogical faith that God can make something out of nothing.

*¹Now **faith** is being sure of what we hope for and certain of what we do not see. ²This is what the ancients were commended for. ³By **faith** we understand that the universe was formed at God's command, so that what is seen was not made out of what was visible.*

Do you believe with certainty that God can create what you hope for out of nothing?

☐ Yes   Why?_____

☐ No   Why not?_____

Thought to Ponder: The universe obeyed God's command. (v. 3)

Two: Have sacrificial faith that pleases God.

*⁴By **faith** Abel offered God a better sacrifice than Cain did. By **faith** he was commended as a righteous man, when God spoke well of his offerings. And by **faith** he still speaks, even though he is dead. ⁵By **faith** Enoch was taken from this life, so that he did not experience death; he could not be found, because God had taken him away. For before he was taken, he was commended as one who pleased God.*

Do you believe that the offering of your life will please God and be commended by him?

☐ Yes   Why?_____

☐ No   Why not?_____

Thought to Ponder: What will your life say to others after you are dead? What legacy of faith are you currently leaving? (vv. 4–5)

Three: **Have expectant faith that God will reward you for seeking him.**

> *⁶And without **faith** it is impossible to please God, because anyone who comes to him must believe that he exists and that he rewards those who earnestly seek him.*

Do you believe that God exists and that he will reward you for earnestly seeking him?

☐ Yes   Why?_____

☐ No   Why not?_____

Thought to Ponder: Do you think you should actually be rewarded for seeking God? (v. 6)

Four: **Have holy-fear faith that condemns evil in the world.**

> *⁷By **faith** Noah, when warned about things not yet seen, in holy fear built an ark to save his family. By his **faith** he condemned the world and became heir of the righteousness that comes by **faith**.*

Do you believe in God strongly enough to have a holy fear of him and look foolish to the world?

☐ Yes   Why?_____

☐ No   Why not?_____

Thought to Ponder: Some believe that Noah had never seen rain. (v. 7)

Five: **Have obedient faith in God's promises to you.**

> *⁸By **faith** Abraham, when called to go to a place he would later receive as his inheritance, obeyed and went, even though he did not know where he was going. ⁹By **faith** he made his home in the promised land like a stranger in a foreign country; he lived in tents, as did Isaac and Jacob, who were heirs with him of the same promise. ¹⁰For he was looking forward to the city with foundations, whose architect and builder is God.*

Do you believe God's promises to you strongly enough to obey and go wherever you are sent, even though you have not clearly been told where you are going?

☐ Yes   Why?_____

☐ No   Why not?_____

Thought to Ponder: Have you created a promised land in your mind with an architect and builder who is *not* God? (v. 10)

Six: **Have unswerving faith in God's future plans for you, even when you are "as good as dead."**

> *¹¹By **faith** Abraham, even though he was past age—and Sarah herself was barren—was enabled to become a father because he considered him **faith**ful who had made the promise. ¹²And so from this one man, and he as good as dead, came descendants as numerous as the stars in the sky and as countless as the sand on the seashore.*

Do you believe that God will be faithful to his future plans for you, even when you feel that you are "as good as dead"?

☐ Yes   Why?_____

☐ No   Why not?_____

Thought to Ponder: Recall when God has been faithful to you in the past. (v. 11)

Seven: Have longing faith to see heaven someday.

*¹³All these people were still living by **faith** when they died. They did not receive the things promised; they only saw them and welcomed them from a distance. And they admitted that they were aliens and strangers on earth. ¹⁴People who say such things show that they are looking for a country of their own. ¹⁵If they had been thinking of the country they had left, they would have had opportunity to return. ¹⁶Instead, they were longing for a better country—a heavenly one. Therefore God is not ashamed to be called their God, for he has prepared a city for them.*

Do you believe that you will see a "better country," a heavenly one?

☐ Yes   Why?_____

☐ No   Why not? _____

Thought to Ponder: Imagine the "better country" God has prepared for you. (v. 16)

Eight: Have undying faith that will survive God's testing.

*¹⁷By **faith** Abraham, when God tested him, offered Isaac as a sacrifice. He who had received the promises was about to sacrifice his one and only son, ¹⁸even though God had said to him, "It is through Isaac that your offspring will be reckoned." ¹⁹Abraham reasoned that God could raise the dead, and figuratively speaking, he did receive Isaac back from death.*

Do you believe that your faith is strong enough to survive God's testing of your trust in him?

☐ Yes   Why?_____

☐ No   Why not? _____

Thought to Ponder: Think about a godly plan you have been tempted to give up on. Could God raise his plan for you from the dead? (v. 19)

Nine: Have publicly-declared faith about the vision God gives you.

*20By **faith** Isaac blessed Jacob and Esau in regard to their future. 21By **faith** Jacob, when he was dying, blessed each of Joseph's sons, and worshiped as he leaned on the top of his staff. 22By **faith** Joseph, when his end was near, spoke about the exodus of the Israelites from Egypt and gave instructions about his bones.*

Do you tell others what God has revealed to you and wants you to share?

☐ Yes Why?_____

☐ No Why not? _____

Thought to Ponder: What would it look like to be a witness to God's faithfulness when your end is near? (v. 22)

Ten: Have fearless faith that invites miracles.

*23By **faith** Moses' parents hid him for three months after he was born, because they saw he was no ordinary child, and they were not afraid of the king's edict.*

Do you believe so strongly that you are unafraid of who or what may attempt to block you from doing God's will?

☐ Yes Why?_____

☐ No Why not? _____

Thought to Ponder: If Moses' parents had let fear control them, God might have allowed Moses to be killed following the king's edict. (v. 23)

Eleven: Have persevering faith in him who is invisible.

*24By **faith** Moses, when he had grown up, refused to be known as the son of Pharaoh's daughter. 25He chose to be mistreated along with the people of God rather than to enjoy the pleasures of sin for a short time. 26He regarded disgrace for the sake of Christ as of greater value than the treasures of Egypt, because he was looking ahead to his reward.*

*²⁷By **faith** he left Egypt, not fearing the king's anger; he persevered because he saw him who is invisible. ²⁸By **faith** he kept the Passover and the sprinkling of blood, so that the destroyer of the firstborn would not touch the firstborn of Israel.*

Do you believe in him who is invisible?

☐ Yes   Why?_____

☐ No   Why not?_____

Thought to Ponder: What causes you to persevere? Is it because you see the invisible God? (v. 27)

Twelve: **Have conquering faith that turns your weakness into strength.**

*²⁹By **faith** the people passed through the Red Sea as on dry land; but when the Egyptians tried to do so, they were drowned. ³⁰By **faith** the walls of Jericho fell, after the people had marched around them for seven days. ³¹By **faith** the prostitute Rahab, because she welcomed the spies, was not killed with those who were disobedient. ³²And what more shall I say? I do not have time to tell about Gideon, Barak, Samson, Jephthah, David, Samuel and the prophets, ³³who through **faith** conquered kingdoms, administered justice, and gained what was promised; who shut the mouths of lions, ³⁴quenched the fury of the flames, and escaped the edge of the sword; whose weakness was turned to strength; and who became powerful in battle and routed foreign armies. ³⁵Women received back their dead, raised to life again.*

Do you believe you will experience the full power of God as you follow his plan for your life?

☐ Yes   Why?_____

☐ No   Why not?_____

Thought to Ponder: Imagine yourself for a moment as an Egyptian drowning in the Red Sea for lack of faith (v. 29), and then as Daniel who, in faith, is shutting the mouths of lions (v. 33).

Thirteen: Have resurrection-faith that withstands persecution.

35Others were tortured and refused to be released, so that they might gain a better resurrection. 36Some faced jeers and flogging, while still others were chained and put in prison. 37They were stoned; they were sawed in two; they were put to death by the sword. They went about in sheepskins and goatskins, destitute, persecuted and mistreated— 38the world was not worthy of them. They wandered in deserts and mountains, and in caves and holes in the ground.

Do you believe strongly enough in God to endure persecution and be willing to die for your beliefs?

☐ Yes   Why?_____

☐ No   Why not?_____

Thought to Ponder: What is the worst physical or emotional harm you have faced because of your faith? If none, recall a time when you stubbed your toe, hit your thumb with a hammer, or were in some other way hurt physically. Would you willingly experience pain or even be willing to die for your beliefs? (vv. 35–38)

Fourteen: Have eternal faith that you will be made perfect with all the saints.

*39These were all commended for their **faith**, yet none of them received what had been promised. 40God had planned something better for us so that only together with us would they be made perfect.*

Do you believe that you will be made perfect with all the saints in eternity?

☐ Yes   Why?_____

☐ No   Why not?_____

Thought to Ponder: The *something better* that God has planned for you includes meeting those who were persecuted for their faith. What will you say to them or ask them when you meet them in heaven? (v. 40)

Read this exercise again in a day or two and reflect on your answers. Feel free to change an answer or add to it.

Conversation Starters about Believe!

- Share your answers and make any comments you would like to make about individual principles and questions.

- Discuss together any insights about your ability or lack of ability to trust in God and believe that he has a plan for your life. In what area do you most need God to increase your faith?

TODAY'S SECOND EXERCISE: FEELINGS YOU MAY HAVE ON THE PATHWAY TO PURPOSE

Walking in faith to discern your purposes and believing against all odds in God's plan for your life isn't always easy. In fact, you may have feelings that surprise you. In this next exercise, check any of the feelings you have had on your journey toward purpose, or write your answer.

FEELINGS I MAY HAVE ON THE PATHWAY TO PURPOSE

Negative Feelings

- ☐ God, you gave me all this work to do and then abandoned me.
- ☐ I can't believe I got myself into this.
- ☐ I can't breathe.
- ☐ I can't do it all.
- ☐ I can't do this.
- ☐ I can't hear you, God.
- ☐ I changed my mind.
- ☐ I don't have time.
- ☐ I feel like I'm in this all alone.
- ☐ I'm exhausted.
- ☐ I'm going to die.
- ☐ I need some help.

Positive Feelings

- ☐ I could work all day (night).
- ☐ I have a place. I fit.
- ☐ I have never felt so peaceful.
- ☐ I have never felt so whole.
- ☐ I have no idea what time it is.
- ☐ I'm finally happy.
- ☐ I'm in my element.
- ☐ I'm in sync.
- ☐ I'm just along for the ride.
- ☐ I'm ready to go.
- ☐ I was born for this.
- ☐ I wish I hadn't wasted so much time on *junk* before this.

(continued)

Negative Feelings (cont.)

☐ I quit.

☐ Lord, I thought you opened doors
and removed barriers.

☐ My heart can't bear the limbo,
not knowing which direction to go.

☐ No, Lord, not that!

☐ Not a crisis now. No, please.

☐ Oh, my head hurts.

☐ This is crazy.

☐ This isn't what I bargained for.

☐ This is too hard.

☐ Why did I ask for this?

☐ Why me, Lord?

☐ Why won't you inspire me, Lord?

☐ You promised to send resources, Lord.

☐ Other: _____

☐ Other: _____

Positive Feelings (cont.)

☐ Life doesn't get any better than this.

☐ Send more work for me to do.

☐ Thank you for letting me serve,
Lord.

☐ Thank you for this privilege.

☐ This is as natural as falling off a
log.

☐ This is fun.

☐ This is me. This is who I am.

☐ That is what life is supposed to be
about.

☐ This is wonderful.

☐ Time just flies.

☐ What an adventure!

☐ What a high.

☐ Other: _____

☐ Other: _____

Conversation Starters about Feelings You May Have:

• Share your answers.

• What surprised you about your answers or shed light on questions you have had?

• Chat about your reaction to the wide variety of feelings you may have as you fulfill God's ultimate plan for your life.

TODAY'S THIRD EXERCISE:
EIGHT PHASES OF GOD'S REVELATION

Even though there are many feelings involved in fulfilling your life purposes, I have observed on my journey with women that there are, typically,
eight phases of a slowly unfolding revelation from God. Check the phase that
best represents where you are currently. If you are in between two phases, put
an X to mark that spot.

EIGHT PHASES OF GOD'S REVELATION

☐ **Calling**   A vague, passionate ache that hovers in your soul as an
impression; sneak previews

☐ **Hoping**   A whispered prayer accepting the call, hoping that you've heard
right

☐ **Doubting**   A serious confusion and questioning

☐ **Believing**   A knowing, a revelation, an epiphany!*

☐ **Doing**   A beginning of countless action steps

☐ **Waiting**   A severe test of patience

☐ **Expecting**   A confidence in God's miraculous power

☐ **Birthing**   A precious gifting of his promise

*Most women do not have an "out of the blue" blinding revelation as did Saul before he
became Paul. Instead, they are given sneak previews and then a clarifying epiphany for
which God has prepared them. (See pages 194–196 in *Pathway to Purpose for Women*
for more about this.)

Conversation Starters about Eight Phases of God's Dream:

- Share your answers about what phase you think you are in. See if your Purpose Partner agrees with you. Discuss your feelings about the phase you are currently in.

- Talk about what you may need to *be* or *do* in order to move to the next phase. By the way, it may be possible that you don't need to *be* or *do* anything, that the ball is in God's court, so to speak! He may want you to wait on his perfect timing, before he moves you to the next phase. The people he is sending you to serve may not be ready for you yet, or he may simply want you to enjoy the roles he has you positioned in right now!

TODAY'S FOURTH EXERCISE: READY, SET, ACTION

I've had clients shake their heads and protest at this juncture, when it actually came time to do something with all the information they had about God's purposes for their lives. But please don't panic. This can be the fun part of the adventure—the initial, short steps before you are expected to take lifelong quantum leaps! Or think of it this way: at least you are moving forward, which can be so much better than the monotony of standing still.

I know it's hard to take action when you can't see the whole picture, but God is notorious for not sharing the whole picture. He wants us to remain dependent on him, learning to trust him more with each step. If you are ready to take some action steps, fill in your responses to the following exercise; then sign it, date it, and ask your Purpose Partner to sign it as well. Then, keep moving forward until God changes your direction. If you aren't ready to take any action steps at this time, think about what might help you change your mind.

MY ACTION STEPS

Based on a great deal of prayer, the encouragement of my Purpose Partner, inspiration from the Holy Spirit, and my own God-given logic, I believe that I am supposed to walk down the particular pathway outlined below to more boldly follow God's purposes for my life. With the help of the Holy Spirit and the prayers of my Purpose Partner, I commit to completing these three action steps in the next three months:

A Great First Step: Within one month, I will _____

_____

A Solid Second Step: Within two months, I will _____

_____

A Tough Third Step: Within three months, I will _____

_____

_____   _____
My Signature   Today's Date

_____   _____
My Purpose Partner's Signature   Today's Date

Conversation Starters about Ready, Set, Action:

- What three action steps did you write?

- Which one do you think will be the most rewarding? Most exciting? Hardest? Easiest?

- Discuss together any insights about the action steps you feel God is asking you to take. Talk to each other about a prayer partnership (via email, letters, or telephone) as you prepare to take your next steps.

Wrapping Up — For the Last Time!

PRAYER LOG:

Update your Prayer Log on page 141 as you share prayer requests and praise reports.

CLOSE YOUR LAST TIME TOGETHER IN CONVERSATION WITH GOD:

Dear God, we want to follow your pathway to purpose, so thank you for your help with this lesson on faith today. Thank you too for helping us understand some of the feelings that surround the discerning of life purposes and some of the many phases we go through in fulfilling your vision. We commit today's action steps to you for your blessing. Thank you for being available to us throughout this entire process. What an honor that you, the King of the universe, would care to spend time with us. In Jesus' name, we pray. Amen.

Purpose Partner Tips

If you are a Purpose Partner who is coaching another woman (also called a *Purpose Partner*!), here are some hints to make your conversations more fruitful:

- It's a good idea to get a workbook for yourself to preview each week, even if you are not going through the exercises yourself. Be prepared for the conversation, at minimum having read through each lesson in advance.
- Pray specifically and regularly about the prayer requests your Purpose Partner shares with you.
- Pray for gentleness, respect, and humility. Mentoring another woman through godly conversations is a privilege that requires gentleness toward her and respect for her, as well as a humble recognition that God has chosen to work through you.
- Pray that God will use you as a change-agent in her life.
- Pray daily about this unique service opportunity and your willingness to "do life together" when appropriate.
- Invite the Holy Spirit to be present at your meetings. Ask for his wisdom and discernment; ask that you will know it is him speaking through you.
- Bring your Bible with you each week and refer to it as your ultimate truth. You may want to familiarize yourself with the index in the back of it, so you can look up topics, if necessary, during your conversations.

- Don't teach or preach. Lead your Purpose Partner to see the truth. Ask questions. Be content to be a coach, mentor, guide, or facilitator.
- Be patient with her by letting her finish her thoughts and by slowing the pace of the conversation if she is wrestling with an idea. Likewise be patient with her character development, her ability to integrate what she is learning, and her willingness to take her next step.
- Remember that God's will is revealed in his time; you do not demand answers from him for your Purpose Partner.
- Be aware of intimidating posture, mannerisms, and language—yours and hers. For example, standing over someone can be interpreted as a power play; crossed arms can signal a closed-minded attitude; a pointed finger can indicate anger; talking fast without eye contact can mean guilt; loudness can mean frustration; and the phrase *you should* often represents a control issue. If you notice any of this behavior, it would be a good idea to chat about it (or confess it) as soon as possible.
- Honor your promise of confidentiality, always resisting the temptation to gossip with or about each other. That is not an option.
- Be authentic; be real. Don't guard every word you speak. Share honestly about your life.
- Commit to the relationship. It will take effort to get to your appointments on time and to stay focused while you are there. If possible, turn your cell phone off while you are meeting. And always end your appointments on time.
- Never worry. God is in control. It's his job to direct your Purpose Partner's steps. Let him.
- Be encouraging and affirming. This will create fertile ground for dreams to sprout.
- Use humor when appropriate. You will be discussing some serious topics and will need to lighten up the conversation from time to time.
- Be a conduit of God's love in the tone of your voice, your inflection, and your willingness to speak truth with love. Remember that God has extended enormous grace to you, and that he wants you to extend grace to your Purpose Partner.

- Leave judgment to God. The minute you become judge and jury for your Purpose Partner, you will lose her emotionally. Your role is to facilitate her processing of ideas, ask questions, listen carefully to her answers, and nudge her along—not judge her.
- Clean up your "own backyard." You don't need to be perfect to fulfill this coaching role, but tell God that you want to be a great role model for your Purpose Partner. Ask him to help you confess and repent of your sins during your relationship. Tell him that you welcome your own spiritual growth and character development.
- Emphasize forgiveness. Your Purpose Partner may need to forgive herself or someone else. Encourage her to do that during your time together.
- Remember to set healthy relational boundaries. Don't create a codependency between you and your Purpose Partner! Ask yourself: *Am I showing empathy, but not taking it to an extreme? Am I encouraging her, but not for the sake of trying to manipulate a response out of her?*
- Help your Purpose Partner see the wide array of opportunities that she might explore. By the way, a woman who has been abused, abandoned, or severely rejected may need some extra help seeing her potential and God's possibilities.

FRESH START WITH JESUS

Therefore God exalted him [Jesus] to the highest place and gave him
the name that is above every name, that at the name of Jesus
every knee should bow, in heaven and on earth
and under the earth, and every tongue confess that Jesus Christ
is Lord, to the glory of God the Father.

(PHILIPPIANS 2:9–11)

Over the course of reading this book, have you agreed to let Jesus be your Savior? If you are ready to take the first step today on the pathway to purpose, here's a simple prayer you can say:

Jesus, I believe that you died for me and that God raised you from the
dead. Please forgive my sins. You are my Savior. You are my only hope.
I want to follow your will for my life. I bow and confess that you, Jesus
Christ, are Lord.

If you decided just now to accept Jesus as your Savior and Lord, you are assured forever of salvation. Nothing can snatch you now from the hand of God. Please let someone know about your decision, so he or she can encourage you and thank God for his grace-filled, purposeful plan for your life.

If you decided not to say the prayer, I urge you to mark this page and to keep seeking truth with an open heart and mind. If you need help, ask a pastor or your Purpose Partner. Some Scripture verses that I highly recommend are these:

Romans 3:23	All have sinned.
Romans 6:23	Heaven is a free gift.
Romans 5:8	Jesus has already, out of love for you, paid the penalty for your sins by dying on the cross.
Romans 10:9–10	If you confess that Jesus is Lord, and if you tell God that you believe he raised Jesus from the dead, you will be saved.
Romans 10:13	Ask God to save you by his grace. He will!

Prayer and Praise Log

Feel free to use this prayer each day (on your own) to pray for your requests and those of your Purpose Partner: *Almighty God, I humbly bow before you as Creator and Ruler of the universe, and I praise you for all you have done for me. I am sorry for my sins, and I ask you to transform me right now to be more like you. Thank you for the insights you have given me so far during this adventure on purposeful living. I desperately need you, and I ask you to take me from where I am today to where you'd like me to be on my journey-to-purpose. I pray specifically and expectantly for these prayer requests that my Purpose Partner and I have listed this week. In Jesus' name, I pray. Amen.*

NOTE: Would you commit some prayer time to asking God if he wants you to become a Purpose Partner for another woman? Can you imagine the woman-power that could be unleashed by you and others who understand the exponential possibilities that begin one woman at a time? Join me in prayer for countless "oaks of righteousness" who will be planted "for the display of the Lord's splendor" (Isaiah 61:3), one woman, one oak, at a time!

Prayer and Praise Log

For Myself and My Purpose Partner

	Prayer Requests and God's Answers	
	Requests:	Answers:
#1 *Conversation*		
#2 *Conversation*		
#3 *Conversation*		
#4 *Conversation*		
#5 *Conversation*		

Prayer Requests and God's Answers	
Requests:	**Answers:**

Conversation #6 *Conversation*
Conversation #7 *Conversation*
Conversation #8 *Conversation*
Conversation #9 *Conversation*
Conversation #10 *Conversation*

ACKNOWLEDGMENTS

I am forever grateful to my son, Andy, who has been my e-commerce consultant, and who constantly asked, "How are you doing, Mom? How can I help?"

To my daughter-in-love, Julie, who is among my greatest cheerleaders, always saying, "I'm so proud of you!"

To my sweet daughter, Steph, who daily inquired, "Do you need anything from the store? Can I get you anything to eat? Can I do that for you?"

I also want to thank the staff administrators at Golden Gate Baptist Theological Seminary on all three California campuses (San Francisco, Brea, and Saddleback Church in Lake Forest) and each of my seminary professors who taught me to think hermeneutically—and who were patient with me when I didn't even come close!

I owe so much to the founder of LifePlanning™, Tom Paterson, who wrote *Living the Life You Were Meant to Live*. Tom and Doug Slaybaugh, a pastor and friend, have both been the Holy Spirit's lifeline to my discovery of my own unique life purpose. And, I'm afraid that I can never fully express my appreciation to Catherine Dubé, who said, "Don't worry, Katie. God is never one second early or late," and to the Saddleback Church Spiritual Growth Team and staff, especially Judy Thompson, Deirdre Cantrell, Anette Rihovsky, Connie Hiss, Dawn Marriccino, Kerri Johnson, Jean Bushong, Terri Haymaker, Mary Scherff, and Pastor Lance Witt. All of them prayed for me on good days and bad.

With indebtedness, I want to thank my agent, Nancy Jernigan, whose incredible vision for the Pathway to Purpose series far surpassed my own; my editor, Cindy Hays Lambert, who is a remarkably gifted writer and tremendously insightful Christian woman. And, the simultaneous release of multiple products never would have happened without the first-class Zondervan team, including Darwin Rader, Greg Stielstra, Greg Clouse, and Autumn Miller— all of whom ministered to me with their kindnesses and expertise. And it was a treasure, indeed, to have the privilege of working on this series with Vicki Cessna, senior public relations manager of Zondervan Trade Books, and Jana Muntsinger and Pamela McClure, the two principals of Muntsinger/McClure Public Relations.

How to Contact the Author

To reach Katie Brazelton, Ph.D,
founder of *Pathway to Purpose*™ *Ministry*,
regarding a speaking engagement,
upcoming seminar,
church consultation,
LifePlan referral or facilitator training,
or to read about her upcoming books
or her dream of opening Women's
Life Purpose Coaching™ Centers,
please visit her website at

www.pathwaytopurpose.com.

Or write to:

Saddleback Church
Katie Brazelton
1 Saddleback Parkway
Lake Forest, CA 92630

To inquire about **any of the women contributors**
in this book series
or to learn more about any of the topics addressed,
please visit the author's website.